PHILIP A. KLEIN
THE PENNSYLVANIA STATE UNIVERSITY

FINANCIAL ADJUSTMENTS

TO

UNEMPLOYMENT

OCCASIONAL PAPER 93

NATIONAL BUREAU OF ECONOMIC RESEARCH
NEW YORK 1965

Distributed by COLUMBIA UNIVERSITY PRESS
LONDON AND NEW YORK

OCCASIONAL PAPER 93

PHILIP A. KLEIN

FINANCIAL
ADJUSTMENTS
TO
UNEMPLOYMENT

NATIONAL BUREAU OF ECONOMIC RESEARCH/1965

RELATION OF THE DIRECTORS TO
THE WORK AND PUBLICATIONS OF THE
NATIONAL BUREAU OF ECONOMIC RESEARCH

1. The object of the National Bureau of Economic Research is to ascertain and to present to the public important economic facts and their interpretation in a scientific and impartial manner. The Board of Directors is charged with the responsibility of ensuring that the work of the National Bureau is carried on in strict conformity with this object.

2. To this end the Board of Directors shall appoint one or more Directors of Research.

3. The Director or Directors of Research shall submit to the members of the Board, or to its Executive Committee, for their formal adoption, all specific proposals concerning researches to be instituted.

4. No report shall be published until the Director or Directors of Research shall have submitted to the Board a summary drawing attention to the character of the data and their utilization in the report, the nature and treatment of the problems involved, the main conclusions, and such other information as in their opinion would serve to determine the suitability of the report for publication in accordance with the principles of the National Bureau.

5. A copy of any manuscript proposed for publication shall also be submitted to each member of the Board. For each manuscript to be so submitted a special committee shall be appointed by the President, or at his designation by the Executive Director, consisting of three Directors selected as nearly as may be one from each general division of the Board. The names of the special manuscript committee shall be stated to each Director when the summary and report described in paragraph (4) are sent to him. It shall be the duty of each member of the committee to read the manuscript. If each member of the special committee signifies his approval within thirty days, the manuscript may be published. If each member of the special committee has not signified his approval within thirty days of the transmittal of the report and manuscript, the Director of Research shall then notify each member of the Board, requesting approval or disapproval of publication, and thirty additional days shall be granted for this purpose. The manuscript shall then not be published unless at least a majority of the entire Board and a two-thirds majority of those members of the Board who shall have voted on the proposal within the time fixed for the receipt of votes on the publication proposed shall have approved.

6. No manuscript may be published, though approved by each member of the special committee, until forty-five days have elapsed from the transmittal of the summary and report. The interval is allowed for the receipt of any memorandum of dissent or reservation, together with a brief statement of his reasons, that any member may wish to express; and such memorandum of dissent or reservation shall be published with the manuscript if he so desires. Publication does not, however, imply that each member of the Board has read the manuscript, or that either members of the Board in general, or of the special committee, have passed upon its validity in every detail.

7. A copy of this resolution shall, unless otherwise determined by the Board, be printed in each copy of every National Bureau book.

(Resolution adopted October 25, 1926,
as revised February 6, 1933, and February 24, 1941)

CONTENTS

TABLES

ACKNOWLEDGMENTS

I AM INDEBTED to Leo Orwicz and R. G. Wagenet of the Bureau of Employment Security, who helped make arrangements for me to obtain the state survey data. For help in acquiring the data themselves, I am grateful to Robert B. Beasley of the Florida Industrial Commission; John W. Bowyer of Washington University, St. Louis; Virlyn A. Boyd, Clemson College; David H. Cameron, Commissioner of the Oregon Department of Employment Security; Abram J. Jaffe of the Institute of Applied Social Research, Columbia University; Keith B. Johnson, Washington University, St. Louis; Helen Kylie, Duquesne University; John S. O'Hara, Florida Industrial Commission; Buford B. Ruhl, Pan-American Consulting Corporation, Miami, Florida; and Wesley E. Zellner, Oregon Unemployment Compensation Commission.

At the National Bureau I have had the advice and assistance of many individuals. Geoffrey H. Moore and Robert P. Shay read the manuscript in several versions and made many helpful suggestions. I am especially grateful to F. Thomas Juster, who not only read the manuscript and suggested improvements but also supervised computations that I was unable to undertake when away from the National Bureau. I am grateful, too, to Arthur F. Burns, Jacob Mincer, Zvi Griliches, Alan Spiro, Victor Zarnowitz, and H. C. Passer, all of whom contributed advice at one stage or another. James F. McRee, Jr., edited the manuscript. The NBER Directors who read this study, Wallace J. Campbell, Marion B. Folsom, and T. O. Yntema, made a number of perceptive and useful suggestions, and it is a pleasure to record my gratitude to them.

Georgette Welscher was my assistant at the Bureau and contributed substantially to the collection and analysis of the basic data. Others who provided valuable assistance include Julia Clones, Bette Fishbein, Susan Fromm, Florence Liang, Martha Jones,

Esther Reichner, and Dora M. Thompson. Muriel DeMar has my special thanks for facilitating my work at the National Bureau in countless ways.

I acknowledge gratefully the help given me by the Advisory Committee of the Consumer Finance Study, which reviewed the findings at several stages and provided a number of useful suggestions: Paul W. McCracken, University of Michigan, chairman; Frank Barsalou, Pacific Finance Corporation; Dorothy S. Brady, University of Pennsylvania; E. Douglas Campbell, Associates Investment Company; John M. Chapman, Columbia University; Mona Dingle, Division of Research and Statistics, Board of Governors of the Federal Reserve System; Bertrand Fox, Harvard University; Raymond W. Goldsmith, Yale University; Robert E. Lewis, First National City Bank of New York; Roger F. Murray, Columbia University; Roland I. Robinson, Michigan State University; Herbert Stein, Committee for Economic Development; Van Buren Thorne, Jr., General Motors Acceptance Corporation; and William L. Wilson, C.I.T. Financial Corporation. Former members of the Advisory Committee include Willcox B. Adsit, George Dimmler, the late George W. Omacht, Sidney E. Rolfe, and LeRoy A. Weller.

A grant to the National Bureau from the International Business Machines Corporation of electronic computer time was utilized for computing the regressions in this study.

This report is part of a broad study of consumer credit being conducted by the National Bureau, made possible by research grants from Associates Investment Company, C.I.T. Financial Corporation, General Motors Acceptance Corporation, and Pacific Finance Corporation. These firms, however, are not responsible for any of the statements made or views expressed in this report.

P. A. K.

FOREWORD

IN THE PLANNING stage of the Consumer Credit Study, some recurrent questions seemed to demand investigation. What happens to consumer debts among households hit by unemployment? Were those who became unemployed more heavily indebted than households in similar economic circumstances whose employment continued? Did the existence of indebtedness cause hardship among the unemployed? Finally, did consumer debt, through its effect upon unemployed households, accentuate business recessions and delay recovery, or did the availability of debt as a means of adjusting to recession offset its deflationary influences?

It was apparent that the relation between indebtedness and unemployment was complicated by other financial adjustments precipitated by changes in household income and expenditures. Hence, in order to analyze the behavior of consumer debt during periods of adversity, it was necessary to adopt a broad approach and study comparatively the expenditure patterns of households with varying amounts of income, debt, and liquid assets. Fortunately, an unusual body of data had become available through the efforts of the U.S. Department of Labor, which had made six regional studies of consumer expenditures of households between 1954 and 1958 in order to ascertain the adequacy of benefits under unemployment compensation systems. These surveys contained a wealth of information about the indebtedness of households experiencing unemployment.

Philip A. Klein's painstaking work on these data has resulted in findings of importance, not only to the objectives of the Consumer Credit Study, but to those interested in the economics of consumption and the impact of unemployment as well. Working closely with F. Thomas Juster, who is conducting a broader study of the effects of credit use upon consumer expenditures, Klein developed empirical evidence to support his major finding that both liquid-asset holdings and consumer debt permit financial adjustments which enable unemployed households to maintain consumption expenditures. He shows that in addition to unemployment benefits, liquid assets primarily and consumer indebtedness to a lesser extent work as compensatory economic stabilizers against deflationary influences among unemployed households.

Klein's insights into debt adjustment patterns among the unemployed permit some further elaboration of the widely held view that cyclical fluctuations in instalment credit are destabilizing. Gottfried Haberler, in his 1942 National Bureau study *Consumer Instalment Credit and Economic Fluctuations,* reached this conclusion and it received further modification and support from Donald M. Humphrey in the Conference on Regulation held in 1956 by the National Bureau (proceedings published in 1957 by the Board of Governors of the Federal Reserve System in its report *Consumer Instalment Credit*). The relevant point made by Klein is that debt adjustments among families hit by unemployment exert a stabilizing influence by moderating the decline in their consumption expenditures. To the extent that this limited stabilizing influence occurs in the general population during recession, it would tend to moderate the general effects of income changes and associated destabilizing changes in the relation between credit extensions and repayments upon consumption expenditures.

Despite the customary difficulties of working with questionnaires designed for a purpose other than the objective of this study, Klein has uncovered many interesting aspects of the relation between unemployment, debt, and expenditures. His work on the debt adjustments undertaken by the unemployed represents, I believe, the first attempt of its kind. His findings, though tentative, are provocative. As a result of his work we have begun to progress beyond everyday notions of what happens to people in debt when they become unemployed.

ROBERT P. SHAY, *Director*
Consumer Credit Study

INTRODUCTION AND
SUMMARY OF FINDINGS

THE HOUSEHOLD confronted with the drastic loss of weekly income that unemployment brings must generally choose between two alternatives: either continuing to spend at its current level by going into debt or using up what it has put aside (that is, allowing its net worth position to deteriorate), or reducing current expenditures and maintaining net worth. To what extent do unemployed persons use these alternatives, and what methods do they use?

This study analyzes the influence on financial adjustments to unemployment of such factors as duration of the out-of-work period, magnitude of weekly income loss during unemployment, asset and debt position of the household at the time unemployment strikes, and the effects of a variety of demographic and other factors on both aggregate and specific adjustments. Financial adjustments are defined as asset, debt, or expenditure adjustments.

CHARACTERISTICS OF THE SAMPLE

The basic data were gathered in six regional unemployment compensation surveys made under the auspices of the Bureau of Employment Security (BES) of the U.S. Department of Labor. Local organizations conducted the surveys in six states from 1954 to 1958. The survey sample consisted of 1,836 persons selected from those applying for unemployment compensation in a given week. The questions asked were retrospective and concerned living arrangements and finances during the year ending with the week of the interview (called the survey year). Interviews typically lasted from two to five hours and sometimes were split into two sessions. The interviewers were trained by the organization delegated by the BES to carry out the survey in each region.

The characteristics of the sample by age, marital status, and occupation groups are in general agreement with Bureau of Labor Statistics nationwide information for the insured unemployed.[1] In comparison with the labor force as a whole, there are relatively fewer very low or very high incomes and fewer very old or very young household heads. What is more significant, perhaps, is that the sample appears to have been more in debt before unemployment than the general population, and to have had smaller liquid assets within each income class. The sample's pattern of expenditure before unemployment was much the same as was that of the population at large. In general, it appears that the sample is sufficiently representative to permit application of the findings of the study to consumers generally, were they to undergo similar experiences.

Summary of Findings

ADJUSTMENTS IN THE AGGREGATE

Households in which a wage earner becomes unemployed have certain broad avenues of adjustment open to them. They can make debt adjustments, expend assets, and cut down expenditures. Or they can encourage other family members to find jobs so as to compensate for the reduced income caused by unemployment.[2]

Net household income of the entire sample decreased during the survey year by an estimated $1,409,000. Earned income dropped by more than that, but was partly offset by unemployment compensation of $648,000. Households adjusted to the decline partly by allowing a deterioration in their net worth, partly by reducing current consumption outlays.

---

[1] Chi-square analysis shows a significant divergence due largely to the underrepresentation of the two youngest age groups in the BES sample. It should also be noted, as Appendix Table A-2 indicates, that the BES sample has relatively more single persons than the BLS sample of the insured unemployed, and fewer widowed or divorced persons. However, the percentage of married persons in the two samples is almost identical.

[2] Labor force participation by household members other than the claimant apparently *decreased* during the period of claimant's unemployment. Earned weekly household income in the sample was less at the end of the survey year than the difference between it and the weekly income earned by the claimant at the beginning of the year. Possibly depressed local conditions resulted in less income-earning opportunities for members of the family other than the claimant.

Net worth adjustments involving debt came to approximately $158,000. Households either increased outstanding debt or postponed repayment of existing debt, and incurred increases of about $83,000 in money loans, $32,000 in unpaid bills, and $43,000 in delinquencies and repossessions on durable goods. Asset holdings were reduced by $322,000, most of it ($261,000) in checking and savings accounts. For the rest of the income loss, $930,000, the households could only reduce consumption expenditures.

The figures have more significance, however, if it is asked what unemployment meant to the individual household. The average net reduction in household income during the survey year amounted to $768—roughly 20 per cent of preunemployment income. Since the period of unemployment averaged just over eighteen weeks, this means the average household lost about $60 a week. Some of this weekly income loss was offset through unemployment compensation payments (about $19 a week). For the rest, the income loss during the survey year was offset by an average debt adjustment of $86 ($5 a week), an average net reduction in assets of $175 ($9 a week), and an average net decrease in expenditures (estimated as a residual) of $506 (or $27 a week). Averages do not tell the whole story because not everyone had assets to fall back on, and debt adjustments were not equally available to all unemployed persons —indeed, for some they were not available at all. In addition, of course, there are differences among households in their preferences for various adjustments.

Role of Debt. During the year in which unemployment occurred, more than one-fourth of the households borrowed money either from family, friends, or financial institutions. Many individuals made use of several kinds of debt in adjusting to unemployment —one could borrow money, run up unpaid bills, default on prior debt obligations, and so on. The ability or willingness to utilize debt tended to increase with both asset holdings and with the duration of unemployment.

Role of Liquid Assets. Liquid-asset holdings were the most important single factor in easing the impact of unemployment on current expenditures. For the sample as a whole, expenditure reduction averaged about two-thirds of the total net income reduction resulting from unemployment; but for those individuals without liquid assets, the reduction in total expenditures averaged about 90 per cent of the net income reduction on the average, compared to a bit over 50 per cent for those who had assets. The reduction in liquid assets held by subgroups of the sample was larger for older age groups up to age 55, and larger for married individuals than for single individuals; among occupational groups, it was largest for professional and managerial persons and smallest for agricultural workers. In all these cases the average change probably reflects the magnitude of liquid asset holdings prior to unemployment, although the data can corroborate this point for only about a fifth of the sample.

Both liquid-asset reductions and debt increases represent a decline in net worth and postponement of reduction in expenditures, and both may be viewed as a way of limiting enforced expenditure reductions in time of unemployment. The data suggest that debt increases constitute a somewhat less important means of adjustment than using liquid assets. Debt adjustments offset 11 per cent of the income change for the entire sample, whereas asset reductions offset 23 per cent. Unemployment-induced debt adjustments tend to be larger for those with outstanding debt prior to the onset of unemployment, primarily because debt adjustments include the failure to repay existing debt as reflected by delinquency and repossession, which tend to be somewhat larger the higher the level of initial debt. Further, consumption expenditures are reduced less, relative to income, the larger the household's initial debt, partly because debt adjustments increase but mainly because liquid-asset reduction is positively correlated with the amount of beginning-year debt. In part, these findings reflect the fact that delinquencies on debt for durable goods are possible only if the household has some of this kind of debt to begin with; families with money loans before unemployment placed less reliance on debt adjustments. It may also be true that these findings reflect differences in preferences among households—those who choose to reduce liquid assets in order to maintain consumption may also be inclined to increase debt (or fail to reduce it as scheduled), relative to those who prefer to reduce consumption and maintain their liquid assets.

RELATIVE IMPORTANCE OF SPECIFIC TYPES OF ADJUSTMENT

Relative importance can be considered either in terms of the number of households that make a particular adjustment or by its dollar amount. By either measure, drawing upon saving and checking accounts is the most important type of adjustment, followed closely by borrowing money and reducing food expenditures. These three are far and away the most important of those considered. The ten other types of adjustment for which both use and dollar volume data were available are given in Table 7.

The findings concerning the importance of liquid-asset holdings in the discussion of aggregate adjustments are supplemented by a more detailed analysis, which indicates that those without liquid assets had less flexibility in adjusting to unemployment-reduced income than did the group with these assets: they were unable to borrow as much, hence reduced their average expenditures for most items to a greater degree. The pattern of relative importance of the specific adjustments is not much altered by the presence of liquid assets, however. Furthermore, it is remarkably pervasive when the sample is subdivided by a variety of demographic and other variables, such as age, occupation, earner status, degree of change in assets, percentage change in income, and location among the six geographical areas from which the samples were drawn. Because some of the six surveys were conducted during periods of recession and others during expansion, the latter finding suggests that the pattern of relative importance may be largely unaffected by the stage of the business cycle during which unemployment occurs.

For the sample as a whole, the data suggest that about one-third of the total income reduction was offset by various kinds of net worth reductions and the remainder by reduction in expenditures. For groups classified by duration of unemployment, the change in expenditure as a proportion of the total *net* change in income (i.e., income earned during unemployment adjusted to include the unemployment compensation payments received) shows that the marginal propensity to consume (MPC) rapidly approaches unity as unemployment continues. By the time people are unemployed for as long as twenty-four weeks, the MPC is more than .95 for those without liquid assets and .73 for those with liquid assets. That is to say, the first group reduced expenditures by 95 cents for every dollar reduction in income and the second by only 73 cents. The MPC is larger for the group without liquid assets unemployed under ten weeks (.79) than it is for the group which has such assets and is unemployed over twenty-four weeks (.73). The net reduction in expenditure is related both to the size of income and income change, as well as to unemployment duration and liquid asset holdings.

While the relative frequency with which alternative adjustments are used is much the same regardless of the period of unemployment, there are nevertheless some differences worth noting. Adjustments which tend to increase most rapidly in the first nineteen weeks of unemployment include delinquencies on rent, major home improvements, appliances, and hospital payments; repossession of appliances; sales of automobiles to raise funds; and decreases in automobile operating expenses. Those which seem to show significantly rapid increase only after twenty weeks of unemployment include delinquencies on mortgages and automobile payments, auto repossessions, and life insurance liquidations.

SOME IMPLICATIONS OF THE FINDINGS

There is evidence of the ability and desire of the unemployed consumer to maintain expenditures, especially for short periods of time, to the extent that liquid-asset holdings and ability to adjust debt make this possible. The findings of this study have implications for assessing the destabilizing consequences of unemployment, particularly unemployment of long duration. Reducing liquid assets and increasing indebtedness (which is more feasible for those with liquid-asset holdings) probably has a smaller destabilizing impact on the economy than does the reduction of consumption expenditures. The latter initiates a chain of consequences which may lead to cumulative contraction. Our estimates of the marginal propensity to consume indicate that the destabilizing influence of unemployment is increasingly serious the longer unemployment lasts, and that liquid-asset holdings contribute a powerful—though temporary—stabilizing influence. Debt adjustment, though quantitatively less important, also acts as a stabilizing (though equally tem- · porary) influence on consumption. Such income supplements as unemployment compensation are quantitatively the most impor- tant stabilizing element, and have the added advantage of not being associated with a deterioration in the net worth position of the household. The average length of unemployment in this sample was slightly over eighteen weeks, and unemployment compensation payments at that time continued generally for twenty-six weeks (fre- quently not beginning for several weeks after the onset of unem- ployment). Again, it is well to bear in mind that the average period of unemployment is the result of unemployment occurring both during periods of expansion and contraction in the economy.

These findings, though tentative because of deficiencies in the basic data, are nonetheless highly suggestive of the factors that have helped to prevent serious recessions in the post-World War II per- iod. Had income supplements not been as large,[3] had the level of liquid assets held by the public not been as high, and had the op- portunities to utilize consumer credit not been as widespread as they were, some of the mild recessions experienced since 1946 might well have developed into more serious recessions or depressions.

[3] If the average period of unemployment had been eight weeks longer, the unemployment compensation component would usually have been used up.

I

CHARACTERISTICS OF
THE SAMPLE AND DATA

THE SIX SURVEYS that provided the underlying data for this study were conducted in Pennsylvania (1954), Florida (1956), South Carolina (1957), New York (1957), Missouri (1958), and Oregon (1958).[1] The data in the six surveys were combined to obtain a sample of

[1] Further information on the area surveys can be obtained from the published summaries of results cited below.

Pennsylvania: 319 respondents, September 1953–August 1954. *A Digest of the Survey of Unemployment Compensation Beneficiaries in Pittsburgh, Pennsylvania*, Duquesne University and U.S. Department of Labor, Bureau of Employment Security, October 1955.

Florida: 273 respondents, November 1955–October 1956. *Unemployment Compensation, A Survey of Benefit Adequacy*, conducted by Pan-American Consulting Corporation, Buford B. Ruhl, president, in cooperation with Florida Industrial Commission and U.S. Department of Labor, June 1957.

South Carolina: 257 respondents, April 1956–March 1957. *Survey of Unemployment Compensation Beneficiaries in Anderson, Greenville, Spartanburg Counties, South Carolina*, conducted by Department of Agricultural Economics and Rural Sociology, Clemson Agricultural College, in cooperation with South Carolina Employment Security Commission and Bureau of Employment Security, U.S. Department of Labor, August 1958.

New York: 269 respondents, May 1956–April 1957. *Benefits, Incomes and Expenditures of Unemployed Workers, Experience of a Group of Unemployment Insurance Beneficiaries in Albany-Schenectady-Troy*, conducted by Bureau of Applied Social Research, Columbia University, under contract with the Division of Employment, New York State Department of Labor, and the U.S. Bureau of Employment Security.

Missouri: 364 respondents, April 1957–March 1958. *Survey of Unemployment Compensation Beneficiaries in St. Louis and St. Louis County*, conducted by School of Business and Public Administration, Washington University, St. Louis, in cooperation with Missouri Division of Employment Security and Bureau of Employment Security, U.S. Department of Labor, June 1959.

Oregon: 354 respondents, April 1957–March 1958. *The Adequacy of Unemployment Benefits, Experience of Unemployment Compensation Beneficiaries in the Portland Metropolitan Area*, by Dr. Carl M. Stevens, Reed College, in cooperation with the Research and Statistics Division, Oregon Unemployment Compensation Commission, Salem, March 1959.

1,836 cases deemed usable. It should be borne in mind that the figures were originally developed to analyze the adequacy of unemployment benefits rather than the pattern of net worth and expenditure adjustment to unemployment; hence the questionnaire was basically concerned with the level of expenditures, income, and so on. Nonetheless, it has been possible to bring the available information to bear on the matter of the nature of unemployment adjustments.

Representativeness of the Sample

The six original subsamples were drawn by means of a survey design developed by the Bureau of Employment Security. The BES sample design did not attempt to garner a random sample; on the contrary, it stratified the sample by selecting only insured unemployed individuals from families of specified composition.[2]

Comparison was made of the BES sample with the Bureau of Labor Statistics' sample of the insured unemployed and also where possible with the total U.S. civilian labor force. The latter comparison is more indicative of differences in the demographic characteristics of the employed and the unemployed generally. The sample was also examined for its representativeness vis-à-vis the insured unemployed with respect to distribution by age, marital status, occupation, disposable personal income prior to unemployment, outstanding debt (by income class and by age), liquid-asset holdings (by income class and by age), and expenditure pattern prior to unemployment.[3] In considering these factors, it should be borne in mind that the sample is stratified by size of household, and so is initially atypical.

The distribution of the BES sample by age and marital status conforms reasonably well to that of the insured unemployed generally. By occupation, too, there is reasonable conformity to the distribution found among the insured unemployed. The greater susceptibility to unemployment of some occupations shows up clearly in

[2] The BES specified that the cases included in the sample should be limited to single persons and persons from four-person households.
[3] Cf. Appendix Tables A-1 to A-7.

the comparison of both the BES and the BLS samples with the employed labor force as a whole.

For the other characteristics no data are available from the BLS sample of all insured unemployed, and the only comparisons possible are between the BES sample and the total U.S. adult population. In the main, the comparisons show the differential impact of unemployment in certain subsectors of the population. Thus, a smaller part of the BES sample comes from upper-income groups since these groups are unemployed with relatively less frequency. The lower-income groups are even more underrepresented, presumably because many low-income agricultural workers, for example, are not eligible for unemployment compensation. It is of interest to note in this connection that the BES sample shows a higher pre-unemployment median income than the population as a whole. In general, it seems to be true that the BES sample of unemployed tends to underrepresent extremes of the population. There are relatively fewer very low or very high incomes, as noted, and also relatively fewer very old or very young family heads.

Much of the subsequent analysis will be concerned with how the unemployed in the BES sample adjusted to unemployment-reduced net family income by utilizing various kinds of debt and liquid assets, and hence it is of interest to know whether or not their pre-unemployment net worth position was in any way unique. Comparison is possible only with consumers in general, but this has some relevance to an analysis of the adjustments that might be expected if unemployment should ever become widespread. Comparison of the BES sample with a sample of all consumers obtained by the Survey Research Center at the University of Michigan suggests that the unemployed in the BES sample are somewhat more likely to be in debt prior to unemployment than the population generally. This is particularly pronounced when one compares respondents with the same income. Only 30 per cent of the entire sample of unemployed had no debt prior to unemployment, whereas the comparable figure for the population as a whole is 41 per cent.[4]

4 Cf. Table A-5. The difference may be because unemployment tends to be repetitive. There were, however, some differences in coverage. Furthermore, there is some evidence that the Survey Research Center makes a less intensive canvass of personal debt than did the BES.

Similarly, there is reason to believe that the percentage in the BES sample with no liquid asset holdings prior to unemployment (43) is higher than that of the population as a whole (26), and that this discrepancy is larger among the upper-income groups.[5] In view of the importance of liquid assets in determining adjustment to unemployment, as will be seen, it is noteworthy that as many as 57 out of every 100 unemployed in the BES sample did have some liquid assets to fall back on.

Inasmuch as we are concerned with how the unemployed in the sample adjusted to their reduced weekly incomes when unemployment struck, it is of interest to know whether their preunemployment expenditure patterns were to any degree dissimilar to the typical expenditure patterns of employed American consumers in recent years. Since studies of all consumers are not frequently conducted, the BES sample was compared with the only general study available for the same period—a study of consumer expenditures undertaken by *Life* magazine. Comparisons are possible only for broad categories of expenditures—food, clothing, home operation, home furnishing, recreation, automobiles, and "other." The two samples show a similar pattern of expenditure. In all income groups food expenditures were the largest item in the family budget in both the BES and the *Life* samples; and while there were differences in relative importance among other adjustments, the rank correlation coefficients were over .9 in all except one income group.[6]

In sum, the BES sample conforms reasonably well to the insured unemployment generally in terms of broad demographic characteristics, allowing for differences in sample design. Differences between the BES sample and the U.S. population reflect the differential impact of unemployment among occupations and income groups. Fi-

---

[5] Cf. Table A-6. Again the data do not permit precise comparisons. Although the definitions of liquid assets used in the Survey Research Center and the BES samples were the same, it was not always possible to distinguish clearly those individuals in the BES sample who had assets from those who had them but did not choose to use them. In other cases individuals would not specify the amount of their asset holdings. A check of one hundred questionnaires from Oregon indicated that only fifteen individuals clearly did not own any liquid assets.

[6] In the under $2,000 income group, the rank correlation coefficient was .7. Cf. Table A-7.

nally, the preunemployment expenditure pattern of the BES sample group suggests that the individuals in the sample were not unique and that other consumers faced with unemployment might be expected to make financial adjustments in roughly similar fashion. It can be concluded that the BES sample is sufficiently representative to permit application of the findings of this study to consumers generally, were they to undergo similar experiences.[7]

[7] However, see Appendix A for a discussion of some other problems which arose in this connection.

II

AGGREGATE ADJUSTMENTS
TO UNEMPLOYMENT

WHEN UNEMPLOYMENT OCCURS, the affected household finds it must adjust to it in a variety of ways. Whether the unemployment was expected or unexpected, as well as the circumstances under which its onset was announced, may affect the way in which the household copes with its problems. Thus a psychological adjustment is required. Unemployment is a social problem as well. Whether it befalls many of one's colleagues, as might be the case during periods of recession, or whether one stands alone in one's group will play a role in the character of adjustment which the affected household will make to the situation.

This study will restrict itself to a consideration of the financial adjustments households make in response to unemployment. Financial adjustments can be defined as those economic adjustments involving debt, assets, and expenditures. Unemployment means, usually, that household income is reduced; in consequence thereof, the customary financial pattern of the household must be reorganized to cope with the unemployment-reduced income. Broadly speaking, therefore, the household's financial adjustment to unemployment involves the manipulation of its asset position, its debt position, and its expenditures to conform to its reduced income.

Expenditures on a variety of goods and services can be reduced. This will affect the customary pattern of living the most in the short run—that is to say, the members of the family will feel the immediate effect on their daily life most intensively. But this adjustment will preserve the family's net worth position. Adjustments affecting the net worth position include incurring new debt, failure to repay existing debt on schedule,[1] and the liquidation of assets, all of which permit the household to reduce current expenditures by less than the loss of weekly income. Deterioration of the household's net worth position is likely to have less destabilizing consequences for the economy as a whole, in the short run, than expenditure reductions have. This is certainly the case for reduction in liquid-asset holdings. It is less clearly applicable to debt adjustments, where the stabilizing influence of expenditure maintenance is offset by the destabilizing consequences of accumulating unpaid bills, delinquencies, and repossessions on both lender confidence and the climate for business investment. In the long run, the prospect of continued impairment of net worth could outweigh the short-run advantages of the maintenance of consumption expenditures.

Ideally, it would be desirable to estimate the total amount of change in liquid assets, debt, and expenditures brought about specifically by the onset of unemployment. Clearly, these magnitudes will change whether or not the household experiences unemployment, and so the unemployment-induced change is not the observed change itself but the difference between the observed change and the "normal" or "customary" change.[2] The survey obtained data on a number of specific changes in expenditures which can reasonably be associated with the onset of unemployment. It seems clear, however, that these changes cannot begin to account for the aggregate change in expenditures brought on by unemployment—probably because those interviewed could not possibly remember in detail their expenditure pattern prior to and during the period of unemployment. Hence, the reliability of the available information varies greatly. Direct information on expenditure change appears

---

[1] Delinquency on existing debt does not of itself impair net worth except to the extent to which interest is allowed to accrue. It does, however, represent a difference between actual and scheduled net worth and thus represents an adjustment to unemployment. The effects of repossession of a durable good on actual net worth are probably zero, since the reduction of assets (the good which has been repossessed) is roughly balanced by the reduction in liabilities that occurs when the debt is extinguished. Repossession can be thought of as equivalent to the forced sale of an asset, therefore, in order to repay debt with negligible effects on the household's net worth.

[2] Cf. Appendix A for a more detailed consideration of this problem.

to be much less reliable than that on changes in debts or assets, for example.

Because changes in debt and liquid assets are more likely to be recorded and to occur in lump-sum amounts after the onset of unemployment, the total change in expenditures has been estimated as a residual. The procedure involves the following steps.

Empirical Estimates

First, the change in net income induced by unemployment was estimated as the algebraic difference between weekly household earnings (take-home pay) at the survey date and weekly earnings prior to unemployment, multiplied by the number of weeks of unemployment; the total amount of unemployment compensation received was then added to the difference in earnings. Mostly the net change was negative, but there were a few cases in which this calculation showed a net increase in household income. Some of these cases are real, since the loss of income from unemployment can be more than offset by unemployment compensation plus increased labor force participation by other family members, but the bulk of them are presumably spurious.[3]

Second, information on debt and asset change was used in order to estimate the unemployment-induced change in net worth. Change in net worth is estimated as the sum of (1) the net change in outstanding (unpaid) bills between the survey date (S_t) and a date one year earlier (S_{t-1}), (2) the net change in personal loans outstanding between S_t and S_{t-1}, (3) the amount of durable goods instalment obligations due between S_t and S_{t-1} that were not paid either because of delinquency or repossession, (4) the net change in checking

[3] There are two basic reasons why the income-change calculation might contain serious errors: (1) household income prior to unemployment might not be adequately measured by the available data, which consist of weekly household income at the beginning of the survey year; (2) the earnings adjustment of the household might not be adequately reflected by the measure used, which is total earnings of all household members at the end of the survey year, i.e., during the week in which the survey was taken. Closely related to the first factor is the implicit assumption that nonlabor income either does not change as a result of unemployment or that any changes which occur are not systematically related to the factors analyzed in this study.

and savings accounts between S_t and S_{t-1}, and (5) the net change in holdings of other assets (life insurance cash value, savings bonds, automobiles) between S_t and S_{t-1}.

Third, the difference between the change in net income and the unemployment-induced change in net worth was taken to be an estimate of the change in consumption expenditures induced by unemployment.

It should be noted that the net worth adjustments listed above do not represent the *actual* change in net worth between S_t and S_{t-1}, but constitute a reasonable estimate of the difference between the scheduled, or "normal," change in net worth and the actual change. All of these adjustments can plausibly be associated with the onset of unemployment, and changes in net worth position that are not a response to unemployment have not been counted as adjustments.[4] For example, individuals who had debt at the beginning of the survey year would be making payments before unemployment, and these decreases in outstanding debt would clearly not be related to unemployment. Similarly, the acquisition of a new durable, such as an automobile, would increase debt outstanding, but would hardly constitute an increase in debt brought on by unemployment. It seemed safe to assume that if major durables were acquired, the acquisition probably occurred during that portion of the survey year which preceded the onset of unemployment, and therefore all new debt secured by durable goods was excluded from the debt-change figure.

On the other hand, if the household borrowed money from any source, it was assumed that all of the increase could be attributed to the onset of unemployment. Since only a few households in the

---

[4] The data suggest that outstanding debt for all families in the sample actually increased by some $20,000 between S_t and S_{t-1}, while our figures show that debt adjustments resulting from unemployment totaled roughly + $157,000. The difference is due mainly to the fact that the actual debt change among sample families included substantial repayments of preunemployment debt on durable goods instalment obligations, and these do not constitute adjustments to unemployment. Durable goods debt is therefore not included. (Because our sample was unemployed, repayments on prior debt would probably have been greater than new durables debt acquired, and so its inclusion would reduce the debt increase.) Another reason for the difference is the inclusion in the debt adjustment total of $43,000 of debt obligation not paid because of either delinquency or repossessions. See note 1.

sample had outstanding money loans at the beginning of the survey year, most such borrowing appears to be associated with unemployment. If bills were permitted to pile up (on food, clothing, rent, and so on), this was also assumed to be an increase in debt related to the onset of unemployment, taking the form of delinquencies on soft goods and services. The failure to meet payments on durables being purchased on credit represents, not an increase in debt, but a manipulation of existing debt (i.e., a failure to reduce actual debt as scheduled). This manipulation was assumed to represent an adjustment to unemployment in the form of durable goods delinquency. Another form of debt manipulation, involving repossessions, actually reduced outstanding debt. If the household permits repossession of durable goods purchased on credit, this conserves whatever sums would have been utilized to make payments on the item being purchased. In consequence of the repossession, these sums can be utilized to maintain expenditures. In all these cases there is, as a result of unemployment, either an increase in debt, a failure to reduce debt as scheduled, or an abandoning of prior debt, and all such adjustments involve the manipulation of debt to free the constrained resources of the household to help maintain expenditure levels.

Table 1 summarizes the major types of net worth adjustments and the residual estimate of consumption expenditure adjustment.[5] Among the various net worth adjustments considered, it is clear that the reduction of checking and savings accounts is of greatest significance. This adjustment accounts for close to a fifth of the entire loss in income. The presence of assets of this magnitude on which to fall back in the face of unemployment is, as we shall see, one of the major determinants of the entire pattern of adjustment which emerges from the present study.

---

[5] The most serious bias in the estimate of net worth adjustment is a probable underestimate of the liquid-asset adjustment. In the postwar period households generally have been increasing their holdings of liquid assets. The actual reduction may therefore tend to understate the unemployment-induced change. The magnitude of the error cannot be sufficient, however, to change any of the basic relations shown by the data. Inasmuch as the error probably lies in the direction of understating the change in liquid assets, the conclusions of the analysis are even more striking.

TABLE 1

UNEMPLOYMENT-INDUCED CHANGES IN INCOME, NET WORTH, AND CONSUMPTION EXPENDITURE OF UNEMPLOYED HOUSEHOLDS

	Aggregate Dollar[a] Amount	Percentage of Total	Average Dollar Amount
Gross reduction in household earnings	2,057,000	--	1,120
Offset through unemployment compensation	648,000	--	353
Net reduction in household income	1,409,000	100	768
Offset through net worth adjustments	479,000	34	261
Debt adjustments	157,000	11	86
Increase in personal loans	83,000	6	45
Increase in unpaid bills	32,000	2	17
Delinquencies and repossessions on instalment obligations	43,000	3	23
Asset adjustments	322,000	23	175
Decrease in checking-saving accounts	261,000	18	142
Decrease in other assets[b]	61,000	4	33
Residual: estimated reduction in consumption expenditure	930,000	66	506

NOTE: Details may not add to totals owing to rounding.
[a] Total number of households in sample is 1,836.
[b] Includes liquidation of life insurance, savings bonds and other similar liquid or semiliquid assets, and the sale of automobiles. While it might be argued that the sale of any durable good would affect the magnitude of the reduction in consumption necessitated by the onset of unemployment, as well as the net worth position of the household, the sale of automobiles was the only such liquidation which was of sufficiently large magnitude and for which sufficiently reliable data were available to warrant its inclusion. In general, the omission of the sale of used appliances and other durable goods should not introduce a significant bias into the residual estimate of consumption.

Among the debt items, the ability to acquire loans from all sources (banks and other financial institutions, family and friends) is the most important, accounting for over half the debt adjustment undertaken and just under 6 per cent of the income lost. Delinquencies in the form of unpaid bills on goods and services and also on durables (including the "savings" realized through nonpayment of existing debt due to repossessions) accounted for the remainder of the contribution made by debt to easing the budgetary constraint imposed on these households by unemployment.

By virtue of the estimates of income change and changes in the rate of accumulation of debts and of assets, consumption expenditure change is estimated (residually) as roughly $930,000, or about two-thirds of the income change. This is the best estimate of the expenditure change occasioned by the loss in income associated with unemployment. However, it must be viewed as no more than a rough approximation because it is subject to the compound errors which are a consequence of the estimating procedure.[6] It should also be noted that unemployment compensation is quantitatively more important than either asset liquidation or debt increase. In addition, resources obtained through unemployment compensation do not cause a deterioration in the household's net worth position as do liquid-asset reductions or debt adjustments.

Limitations of Estimates

While the estimate of expenditure change here is by no means precise, it appears to be a better estimate of total change than any which can be extracted from the original data on expenditures. Some of the more important components of the total expenditure change are reported in sufficient detail to be usable by themselves, and they are examined below. But the reported information on expenditure adjustments as a whole must be viewed as inadequate. It is impossible to account for anything like the estimated decrease in income by adding up all the debt, liquid-asset, and expenditure changes which have been included in the detailed questionnaire from which the basic data for this study were obtained. Although there are difficulties with the other variables, examination of the data demonstrates convincingly that the basic difficulty lies with the expenditure data.[7] The interviewee had bankbooks, canceled

[6] If the components of net worth adjustment are in error but the errors tend to cancel, there is no bias in the residual estimate of consumption. But if either the income change or net worth change estimates are in error, consumption change has an error equal in absolute size.

[7] The unemployment-induced change in expenditure can be computed for a class of items in the survey which appears to comprise approximately 50 per cent of total expenditure. (Expenditure change for such items as clothing, medical expenditures, durable goods, recreation, etc., cannot be estimated with any reliability at all.) It was then assumed that total expenditures changed by the same percentage as the classes of expenditures for which unemployment-induced change could be estimated. Such a calculation was made for each household, and the resulting estimate of total unemployment-induced expenditure change was then compared with the residual estimate of change described above. The

checks, and numerous other evidence of debt and asset change to help his memory. While there is, of course, no way of knowing whether or to what degree the interviewees utilized such information, it is nevertheless important to note that this sort of evidence would not generally even be available for estimating many parts of expenditure change.[8] On the other side, however, one might argue that survey respondents have generally shown a greater reluctance to provide information about assets and debts than about expenditures.

Analysis of Aggregate Adjustments

As Table 1 indicates, the reduction in consumption constitutes about two-thirds of the reduction in income. In effect this constitutes an empirical estimate of the marginal propensity to consume (MPC) for the sample as a whole. We shall have occasion to consider the effect of a variety of other variables on this estimated marginal propensity to consume. An estimated MPC of .66 appears to be quite low—for the economy as a whole during recent years, the MPC averages about .93. However, the latter figure is not based on conditions of widespread income decline. Comparison of per capita disposable income with per capita consumption for the United States (1962 prices) for the years 1929–62 shows eleven years in which income declined from the preceding year. The

change in total expenditures based on extrapolation of apparent change for specific items was so small, and the correlation between direct and residual estimates was so low (.0003), that we decided to ignore the direct estimate of expenditure change and accept the residual estimate, which, whatever its shortcomings, seems to be the better one.

[8] The survey procedures included a check on the accuracy of the data by examination of the discrepancies between total receipts and total outlays, termed a "balancing difference." Whenever this difference was greater than one-third of the reported change in income, the questionnaire was discarded. In the South Carolina survey this technique was employed with notable care. Each questionnaire had appended to it a balancing-difference worksheet on which total financial resources (income), as adjusted for changes in debt and assets, was balanced against the total reported expenditures for the year. The percentage variation between the total annual (adjusted) income and the total reported annual expenditures was calculated; if the difference was more than 33 per cent of the smaller figure, the data were rechecked. If the difference remained the interview was not used. Even so, differences as great as one-third could and did remain in the final sample.

MPC's vary widely from 1.1 (expenditures decline more than income) to a negative number (expenditures increase when income
decreases). The median MPC for these eleven years is .64, quite
close to the estimate in our sample.[9] Further, the median figure,
.64, is for 1931–32, and this is the only period in which income
declined enough so that aggregate national savings went from a
positive to a negative figure. The situation then was somewhat
similar to that prevailing in the sample, in which all the individuals
were unemployed and savings became negative. In 1931 and 1932
the country was in the depths of the depression, unemployment
was widespread, adjustments to reduced income needed to be made
most acutely, and assets declined most sharply. The figures suggest,
therefore, that the relation between expenditure adjustment and
income change in the sample is not unreasonable as an indication
of the impact of unemployment.

While the aggregate dollar figures in Table 1 provide a conven-
ient summary of the major adjustments undertaken by the entire
sample, they should also be considered in terms of what they meant
for the average household. The third column of the table shows
the average change during the survey year in each of the major
adjustment categories for the households included in the sample.[10]
It must be borne in mind that these are *net* figures—the "average"
income loss includes, for example, households which increased income despite unemployment. With unemployment averaging a bit
over eighteen weeks for the entire sample, weekly net income loss
averages about $41. Since unemployment compensation is included
in the income figures, net earned income actually declined about
$19 more—the average weekly amount of unemployment compen-

9 Cf. *The Economic Report of the President,* January 1963, p. 191, for
the data from which the MPC's were computed. The years in which income
declined and the computed MPC's are: 1929–30, + .90; 1930–31, + .82; 1931–32,
+ .64; 1932–33, + 1.00; 1937–38, + .38; 1944–45, – 1.97; 1945–46, – 4.11; 1946–47,
+ .04; 1948–49, – 1.10; 1953–54, + .39; 1957–58, + 1.08.

10 These simple averages are useful for initial consideration of individual
adjustments to income reduced by unemployment. However, all individuals in
the sample could not take advantage of all these major adjustment techniques,
and so more meaningful averages will necessitate confining the cases to those
who actually could avail themselves of each technique. The problem is considered in the next section, in which all these magnitudes are disaggregated
where possible.

sation received by sample households during the period of their unemployment.[11] Thus weekly earned income declined by about $60 on the average. The average weekly adjustments included about $19 in unemployment compensation, $27 in expenditure reductions, $5 in debt increases, and $9 in asset reductions. The expenditure reduction was, then, less than half the decline in earned income. Though these estimates may be more than usually prone to the errors inherent in interpreting averages, they do give a rough indication of the relative importance of the various major avenues of adjustment used by typical American households forced to cope with unemployment.

Impact of Duration of Unemployment

The pattern of aggregate adjustment will obviously be significantly different for some households than for others, and it might be supposed that unemployment of increasingly long duration would materially affect the relative importance of the major adjustive techniques. In Table 2 the sample has been classified according to duration of unemployment, and the aggregate debt, liquid asset, and expenditure adjustments are shown.

A word of explanation is in order concerning the group in Table 2 unemployed over twenty-four weeks. Inasmuch as unemployment pensation benefits during the period covered by the surveys rarely were paid for periods longer than twenty-six weeks, many of the 439 individuals included in this category must either have been unemployed more than once during the survey year (so that the total weeks of unemployment came to more than twenty-six) or have failed, for some reason, to apply immediately for benefits. In either event, the behavior pattern of many in this group can be expected to diverge from that of the rest of the people.

Further, adjustment categories where the aggregate had to be

[11] It is interesting to note that sample households received unemployment compensation for a period that averaged about twelve weeks, while unemployment itself averaged about eighteen weeks. This is the reason why the "average" weekly amount of unemployment compensation was only about $19. The discrepancy no doubt reflects the "waiting period" between the application for and receipt of unemployment compensation payments, but the discrepancy is much larger than can be accounted for by this factor alone.

TABLE 2

Unemployment-Induced Changes in Income, Expenditure, Debt, and Liquid Assets, by Duration of Unemployment

Duration of Unemployment (weeks)	Number in Sample (1)	Avg. Wks. of Unemployment (2)	Income		Consumption Expenditures		Debt Adjustment		Liquid Asset Adjustment		Estimated Marginal Propensity to Consume (11)	Estimated Marginal Propensity to Dissave (12)
			Total (3)	Wky. (4)	Total (5)	Wky. (6)	Total (7)	Wky. (8)	Total (9)	Wky. (10)		
0–9	292	7	324	46	106	15	77	11	142	20	.33	.67
10–14	397	12	480	40	260	22	102	8	118	10	.54	.46
15–19	387	17	697	41	401	24	78	5	219	13	.57	.43
20–24	321	22	888	40	648	29	100	5	140	6	.73	.27
Over 24	439	31	1,297	42	1,077	35	73	2	146	5	.83	.17
Total	1,836	19	768	40	528	28	86	5	154	8	.69	.31

(Column header note: columns 3–10 fall under "AVERAGE DOLLAR REDUCTION IN:" for Income and Consumption Expenditures, and "AVERAGE DOLLAR OFFSET TO INCOME REDUCTION THROUGH:" for Debt Adjustment and Liquid Asset Adjustment.)

NOTE: For the estimating procedures used to obtain the data in columns 3–10, see text. Column 11 is column 5 divided by column 3; column 12 is the sum of columns 7 and 9 divided by column 3. In columns 3, 5, 7, and 9 the numbers represent average change during the entire period of unemployment. Columns 4, 6, 8, and 10, marked "weekly," indicate the average weekly change during the period of unemployment.

extrapolated from a sample of cases in which dollar amounts were provided—liquidating life insurance and selling cars—are not included in the calculation. Hence the total asset reduction shown in Table 2 is lower than in Table 1, and the residual estimate of consumption change is correspondingly a smaller number (algebraically). This difference has no substantive influence on the pattern of adjustment.

As one would expect, the average income reduction increases steadily as unemployment is prolonged, as does the average dollar reduction in consumption expenditures. The residual change in expenditure not only increases in absolute terms but increases also as a percentage of the income reduction. Only about one-third of the income loss is met through expenditure reduction, on the average, in the initial stages of unemployment. By the time individuals are unemployed for as long as twenty-four weeks, about three-quarters of the household's total income loss is met by expenditure reductions.

As has been stated, the adjustments to unemployment which reduce net worth are less painful in the short run, but are probably more severe in their long-run consequences. By the same token, reduced consumption expenditures have greater immediate impact both on short-run living standards and economic stability. It is a commonplace of economic analysis that expenditure changes have derivative consequences which depend upon the size of the marginal propensity to consume. In the sample, then, the fact that the MPC rises steadily means that the consequences of unemployment become increasingly severe for the economy as the average duration of unemployment rises even if the level of unemployment remains the same.

Debt and Asset Adjustments

Tables 3 and 4 indicate total and average dollar adjustments for the major-debt and liquid-asset categories respectively, as well as the percentage of income change represented by each. From the last column in Table 3, it is clear that the average amount of debt

TABLE 3
UNEMPLOYMENT-INDUCED CHANGES IN INCOME, TOTAL DEBT, AND DEBT COMPONENTS, BY DURATION OF UNEMPLOYMENT

Duration of Unemployment (weeks)	Number in Sample	Dollar Amount of Change in:				
		Total Household Income	Money Loans	Unpaid Bills	Repossession and Delinquency on Durables	Total Debt
ACGREGATE CHANGE						
0–9	292	−94,741	16,018	3,276	3,134	22,428
10–14	397	−190,498	22,358	8,151	9,955	40,464
15–19	387	−269,894	14,172	6,939	8,888	29,999
20–24	321	−284,990	13,457	6,564	12,057	32,078
Over 24	439	−569,213	16,633	6,742	8,836	32,211
Total	1,836	−1,409,336	82,638	31,672	42,870	157,180
AVERAGE CHANGE						
0–9	292	−324	55	11	11	77
10–14	397	−480	56	21	25	102
15–19	387	−697	37	18	23	78
20–24	321	−888	42	20	38	100
Over 24	439	−1,297	38	15	20	73
Total	1,836	−768	45	17	23	86
PERCENTAGE OF INCOME CHANGE						
0–9	292	100	17	3	3	24
10–14	397	100	12	4	5	21
15–19	387	100	5	3	3	11
20–24	321	100	5	2	4	11
Over 24	439	100	3	1	2	06
Total	1,836	100	6	2	3	11

NOTE: All estimates are net—that is, increases and decreases are added algebraically. Details may not add to totals owing to rounding.

adjustment (in dollars) does not vary systematically with the duration of unemployment. Resort to money loans lessens somewhat as duration increases: people borrow relatively early and then must either repay the initial loans or encounter increasing difficulty in obtaining additional loans. Thus the average amount of loans declines from over $50 during short periods of unemployment to under $40 for periods of longer unemployment. By the same token, however, the average dollar change in delinquencies rises irregularly. Among debt adjustments, therefore, the initially greater reliance on money loans is rapidly diminished so that it is not very

TABLE 4

UNEMPLOYMENT-INDUCED CHANGES IN INCOME, TOTAL LIQUID ASSETS, AND LIQUID-ASSET COMPONENTS, BY DURATION OF UNEMPLOYMENT

Duration of Unemployment (weeks)	Number in Sample	Household Income	Checking and Savings Accounts	Other Liquid Assets	Total Liquid Assets[a]
			Dollar Amount of Change in:		
		AGGREGATE CHANGE			
0-9	292	-94,741	-40,858	-521	-41,379
10-14	397	-190,498	-39,156	-7,818	-46,974
15-19	387	-269,894	-79,353	-5,512	-84,865
20-24	321	-284,990	-38,211	-6,703	-44,914
Over 24	439	-569,213	-63,622	-393	-64,015
Total	1,836	-1,409,336	-261,200	-20,974	-282,174
		AVERAGE CHANGE			
0-9	292	-324	-140	-2	-142
10-14	397	-480	-99	-20	-118
15-19	387	-697	-205	-14	-219
20-24	321	-888	-119	-21	-140
Over 24	439	-1,297	-145	-1	-146
Total	1,836	-768	-142	-11	-154
		PERCENTAGE OF INCOME CHANGE			
0-9	292	100	43	1	44
10-14	397	100	21	4	25
15-19	387	100	29	2	31
20-24	321	100	13	2	16
Over 24	439	100	11	0	11
Total	1,836	100	18	2	20

NOTE: Details may not add to totals owing to rounding.

[a] Total liquid-asset change as measured here does not include liquidation of life insurance, as noted in the text.

much more important than the other categories after unemployment has continued for fifteen weeks.[12] Finally, the percentage of total income change offset by debt adjustments becomes steadily less important as unemployment lengthens, mainly because the income reductions become larger.

[12] It has been possible to construct more precise tests of these aggregate relations with data collected only in the Pittsburgh survey. The primary analytical advantage of the 319 cases in the Pittsburgh area (which constituted the pilot study for the Bureau of Employment Security) is that, in addition to data on changes in debts and liquid assets, information was also acquired on the *levels* of these variables at the beginning of the survey year. This is examined below.

Table 4 summarizes the relevant information relating the duration of unemployment to the utilization of liquid assets as an offset to income reduction. Again, there appears to be no particular pattern to the average dollar volume in the successive duration classes. This impression may be misleading, however. In the Pittsburgh sample, where data are available on the level of beginning-year liquid assets, it is clear that a larger proportion of assets are used up as duration lengthens. (See Table 11.) By the time people are unemployed for as long as twenty-four weeks, liquid assets are generally used up completely, suggesting that the data in Table 4 fail to show an increase in the average amount of asset reduction because preunemployment asset holdings are markedly smaller in the long-duration groups. It is possible, for example, that the duration of unemployment is correlated with the frequency of previous unemployment.

It is also possible that the data in Table 4 reflect the fact that unemployment was anticipated to a greater degree by those out of work for longer periods. If so, liquid-asset holdings may have been increased during the survey year prior to the start of unemployment. But the data measure the difference between assets at the beginning and end of the survey year, not between peak holdings prior to unemployment and end-of-year holdings.

The relation between duration of unemployment and adjustment to it is most clearly shown in Table 5, which summarizes the per-

TABLE 5

MAJOR ADJUSTMENTS TO INCOME REDUCED BY UNEMPLOYMENT

Duration of Unemployment (weeks)	Number in Sample	Percentage of Income Loss in Form of:			
		Expenditure Adjustment	Debt Adjustment	Liquid-Asset Adjustment	Total
0–9	292	33	24	44	100
10–14	397	54	21	25	100
15–19	387	57	11	31	100
20–24	321	73	11	16	100
Over 24	439	83	06	11	100
Total	1,836	69	11	20	100

NOTE: Details may not add to totals owing to rounding.

centage of income change in each unemployment duration class which is offset by changes in each of the three broad categories. The expenditure adjustment is the estimated marginal propensity to consume for each class. The debt and liquid-asset adjustments represent the two components of the marginal propensity to dissave. Two conclusions stand out clearly: (1) In the early part of a period of employment, the use of both liquid assets and debt generally holds down reductions in expenditure; but as the period of unemployment lengthens, an increasing fraction of the income loss is met by such a reduction.[13] (2) Liquid-asset reductions constitute a more important means of maintaining current consumption than do debt increases.

Finally, it is worth noting that these findings are consistent with a number of hypotheses about the relation between current income and expenditures for current consumption. The evidence suggests that unemployed individuals attempt to maintain expenditures at levels commensurate with their customary level of income, utilizing both available assets and debt in order to maintain consumption levels. The hypotheses associated with Duesenberry, Friedman, and Mack are all consistent with this finding.[14]

[13] In the Pittsburgh sample, income prior to unemployment and unemployment duration are statistically significant determinants of the change in consumption, as is the interaction of duration with the level of beginning-year loans.

[14] See James S. Duesenberry, *Income, Saving, and the Theory of Consumer Behavior*, Cambridge, Mass., 1949; Milton Friedman, *A Theory of the Consumption Function*, Princeton University Press for NBER, 1957; and Ruth P. Mack, "The Direction of Change in Income and the Consumption Function," *Review of Economics and Statistics*, November 1948.

III

SPECIFIC ADJUSTMENTS

TO UNEMPLOYMENT

THERE ARE A NUMBER of categories of expenditure adjustment for which reasonably reliable data are available. This section examines the relative importance of these adjustments as well as the importance of some specific asset and debt adjustments. In addition it examines the changing reliance of the unemployed upon these alternative adjustments as the period lengthens.[1]

There are two ways of measuring relative importance. The first is by the dollar volume represented by a given adjustment, the second by the number of people who utilized the adjustment. Since frequency of use is undeniably the easiest measure to acquire, we possess such data for a much larger number of adjustments than those for which reasonably accurate dollar-volume estimates could be constructed. But the problem faced by the unemployed is ultimately a dollar problem. Income is lost by virtue of unemployment; the problem is to compensate for the dollar loss either by reducing dollar outlay or by acquiring dollars from some nonincome source. Analytically, therefore, there is much to be said for attempting to measure the importance of various adjustments in terms of dollar volume, and this has been done wherever possible.[2]

[1] The original questionnaires yielded a list of forty-seven variables representing changes in the household's financial position which could reflect possible adjustments to unemployment, but only a limited number actually showed significant relations to unemployment. In addition, as indicated in the text, information on some of the important adjustments was fragmentary or inadequate. The complete list appears in Appendix B. The list of adjustments analyzed here involves most, but not all, techniques used by at least 1 per cent of the sample.

[2] All other information on dollar adjustment has been computed in similar fashion to that of the total dollar-income loss, previously explained. Weekly

In comparing dollar-volume estimates analyzed here with those in the previous section, it must be borne in mind that the figures in Section II were all net, i.e., debt increase less debt decrease; whereas the present discussion revolves about the gross figures, i.e., the absolute amount of debt increase for those who increased debt.

Relative Importance of Adjustive Techniques Measured by Frequency of Use

Frequency of use can be measured by relating the number of users of a given technique to the total number of households in the sample. Alternatively, the denominator can be restricted to the number of individuals who could have used the technique. In some cases these two alternatives yield the same result; all households in the sample had expenditures for food and so all could conceivably have reduced them. However, only smokers, for example, could have reduced tobacco expenditures and only renters could have permitted rents to become delinquent. Table 6 gives both sets of percentages. The percentage of possible users who utilized each technique (third column) seems the best standard of importance in terms of frequency, and for the most part this measure is used here.[3]

Table 6 represents those techniques of the forty-seven listed in Appendix B for which the data seemed sufficiently reliable and the importance sufficiently prominent to warrant analysis. The most striking feature of these data is the outstanding importance attached to reducing checking and savings accounts. More people by far adjusted to the budgetary constraints brought on by unemployment in this way than in any other—and by a substantial margin.

The importance of both borrowing money and reducing food expenditures is also noteworthy. We have previously indicated (Table 3) the kinds of debt adjustments included in borrowing money. It remains, therefore, to indicate, to the limited extent possible,

---

or monthly data on differences between preunemployment and during-unemployment expenditures have been weighted by the number of weeks or months of the survey year during which the interviewees were unemployed.

[3] In this respect the present discussion differs from the aggregate analysis above, where averages were based on the entire sample. But only those who possessed liquid assets could have utilized them. In a subsequent section, we shall take this into account by disaggregating the sample.

TABLE 6

PRINCIPAL TECHNIQUES OF ADJUSTMENT TO UNEMPLOYMENT

Adjustment Technique	Persons Using Technique (1)	Number of Users as Percentage of: Total Sample (2)	Number of Users as Percentage of: Possible Users (3)	Rank of Column 3 (4)
Decrease savings and checking accounts	737	40.1	74.1[a]	1
Decrease food expenditures	476	25.9	25.9[b]	4.5
Borrow money (all sources)	476	25.9	25.9	4.5
Drop hospital plans[c]	433	23.6	32.5	2
Decrease amount spent on car operation	164	8.9	19.8[d]	7
Permit delinquent rent	135	7.4	14.0	8
Permit delinquent payments on:				
Appliances purchased, survey year	131	7.1	22.4	6
Appliances purchased before survey	116	6.3	29.2	3
Liquidate life insurance[e]	115	6.3	9.5	11
Decrease liquor expenditures	95	5.2	11.0[f]	9
Sell car	93	5.1	7.2	12
Permit delinquent hospital insurance	79	4.3	5.9	13
Decrease tobacco expenditures	51	2.8	3.7[g]	16
Permit delinquent payments on car purchased, survey year	47	2.6	9.7	10
Permit repossession of car	46	2.5	5.6	14
Permit repossession of appliance	21	1.1	2.1	18
Renew or refinance mortgage	18	1.0	4.9	15
Permit delinquent payments on major home improvement	16	0.9	2.8	17

[a] This figure is doubtless overstated. Only 994 of the 1,836 households in the sample clearly indicated that they had checking or savings accounts by reporting that they increased or decreased them. The questionnaires were ambiguous as to whether the remaining households had no checking or savings accounts, or had them but left them intact. A careful hand sampling of 100 cases from the Oregon sample indicated that 85 per cent of these respondents actually seemed to have either a checking or a savings account, instead of the 54 per cent implied by the above data. If so, the percentage of possible users who reduced checking and savings accounts would presumably be less than 74 per cent, although it is impossible to say how much less.

[b] 13.1 per cent of all cases increased food expenditures.

[c] The prominent position given to this type of adjustment must be interpreted with caution. Cf. the discussion in the text.

[d] 7.5 per cent of all cases increased the amount spent on automobile operation.

[e] This question was not asked in the Pittsburgh survey. If the 115 users are adjusted to include an estimate for the Pittsburgh sample, the number of users is increased by the ratio of Pittsburgh to non-Pittsburgh cases (319:1517), yielding a total of 139 users. This adjustment will not change the percentage of possible users, because both the numerator and denominator will be adjusted by this same factor. It will change the percentage of all cases (to just under 8 per cent). Inasmuch as the latter measure will not be utilized in the subsequent discussion, this adjustment is not included in the table.

[f] 2.3 per cent of all cases increased liquor expenditures.

[g] 1.2 per cent of all cases increased tobacco expenditures.

the nature of the reductions in food expenditures. Because these expenditures bulk large in every household budget, they are an obvious avenue through which to attempt to adjust the household budget to unemployment-reduced income. It is, however, not possible from the data available in this area to specify in detail what sort of expenditures were reduced. Much of it was probably a reduction in expenditures for quality foods, though how much may also have been a reduction in total food intake is impossible to say. Inasmuch as eating in restaurants may well have been viewed as a form of recreation, it may have been included in the recreation category rather than in food expenditures.

The apparent prominence given to dropping hospital plans is misleading. Of the 433 individuals who dropped them, only 54 had individually arranged plans. The rest represent a wide variety. Some were plans in which the costs were deducted from wages and salaries, some included payments made by employers, and so on. In many cases, therefore, there would have been a substantial increase in cost to the individual had he attempted to take over the entire burden of payments for himself. In the case of noncontributory company health plans, of course, becoming unemployed meant compulsory dropping of the health plan as well. (The adjustment involved in permitting delinquencies to develop on hospital insurance is far less important since it is restricted to individually arranged policies involving both relatively small amounts and relatively few people.) Nonetheless, these figures provide impressive evidence that one of the by-products of unemployment is to increase the vulnerability of the affected individuals to any medical expenses which may be incurred. This vulnerability is further affected by the loss of other fringe benefits (i.e., life insurance, free medical care, use of recreation facilities) which frequently accompany unemployment.

It will be noted that mortgage refinancing was infrequently utilized. The reason undoubtedly lies in the fact that many mortgages, especially FHA mortgages, do not permit refinancing, and so what would otherwise appear to be a promising avenue of adjustment to reduced incomes is blocked. To some extent, households that managed to borrow money through mortgage refinancing may have been included in the "borrow money (all sources)" category.

A final point has to do with the universality of the pattern of relative importance indicated by the above data. We disaggregated the sample by such characteristics as age, occupation, earner status,[4] the dollar change in liquid assets during the survey year, the percentage change in annual income resulting from unemployment, and the geographical location (state) where the interview was obtained. The results suggest that the pattern of relative importance is remarkably pervasive. (See Table A-8, below). In almost all cases the Spearman rank correlation coefficient between the pattern for the individual group and that for the entire sample was above .90. In a few more it was in the high .80's. Only in one case was the pattern of relative importance significantly divergent. For those whose liquid assets during the survey year increased by more than $1,000—surely an atypical group of unemployed persons—the rank correlation coefficient was in the .50's. There were other discrepancies: the professional and managerial group had a rank correlation coefficient in the .70's, no doubt reflecting their tendency to have larger liquid-asset holdings as well as higher incomes; Pennsylvania had a lower correlation coefficient, owing perhaps to its position as an area of chronic unemployment. In general, the evidence indicated that all unemployed persons, regardless of demographic or other differences, utilized these adjustments with roughly the same relative frequency. The differences which show up usually reflect either differences in liquid-asset holdings or in ability to incur new debt, to both of which attention will be directed shortly.

Relative Importance of Adjustive Techniques Measured by Dollar Volume

Table 7 indicates the dollar volume of gross adjustment made in thirteen areas for which reasonably accurate information was available or could be estimated. The pattern of relative importance can be seen in terms of dollar volume and relative frequency. The most striking feature of the table is the dominant importance of the net worth adjustments, measured either by dollar amount or relative

---

4 The three categories utilized here included single earners, married earners who were the primary earner in the family, and married earners who were secondary earners (i.e., not head of the household).

TABLE 7

TOTAL DOLLAR AMOUNTS INVOLVED IN THIRTEEN TECHNIQUES

OF ADJUSTMENT TO UNEMPLOYMENT

Adjustment Technique	Estimated Gross Dollar Amount[a]	Percentage of Possible Users
1. Decrease savings and checking accounts	349,990	74.1
2. Borrow money (all sources)	196,995	25.9
3. Decrease food expenditures	62,400	25.9
4. Cash in savings bonds	30,000[b]	n.a.
5. Permit delinquent payments on appliances purchased	27,000[c]	26.0
6. Sell car	25,000[d]	7.2
7. Liquidate life insurance	21,000[e]	9.5
8. Savings through repossessions (all items)	9,500[f]	4.0
9. Permit delinquent rent	9,455	14.0
10. Decrease amount spent on car operation	8,723	19.8
11. Permit delinquent payments on car purchased	6,420	9.7
12. Decrease liquor expenditures	6,044	11.0
13. Decrease tobacco expenditures	1,297	3.7
Total	753,824	

NOTE: Net worth adjustments = $675,360 (89.6 per cent); expenditure adjustments = $78,464 (10.4 per cent).

[a] This column shows gross estimates of the adjustments for which presumably accurate totals were available, and also those for which reasonably accurate estimates were possible. See the following notes.

[b] Information on savings bonds was not obtained in Pittsburgh, although there is reason to believe that the bulk of the "other asset" category there was largely bonds. Total sales of bonds by the 1,517 cases in other localities in the sample came to $25,449. Inasmuch as Pittsburgh's 319 cases comprise 17.4 per cent of the entire sample, the bond figure was adjusted to give an estimated figure of $30,000. The reader is again reminded that these figures are all gross.

[c] An estimate of delinquencies on autos is subtracted from the known total delinquency figure ($33,352) to get the total appliance delinquency estimate of $26,932; the latter has been rounded in the table.

[d] Of the 93 known cases here, dollar amounts were available for 67, totaling $17,642. On the assumption that average price received was the same for the 26 missing amount cases as for the 67 cases with known amounts, $24,487 is the estimated total. This figure has been rounded.

[e] The life insurance figure has been adjusted to include the Pittsburgh figures, using the same procedure as in note b, and to reflect the fact that some households did not report dollar amounts but simply liquidation.

[f] Average monthly repayments during the survey year, plus the month in which repossession occurred, enable estimation of the saving through repossession. The figure represents forgone payments each month, which eases the family budget by ceasing to constitute a claim against the now reduced family income.

frequency of use. The decrease in liquid assets (almost $350,000) represented a far larger amount than that for any other adjustment. In the absence of liquid-asset holdings the expenditure reductions would perforce have been much greater. (Whether they would also have been different is the subject of the next section, in which adjustments for households with no liquid assets holdings prior to unemployment are examined.)

Almost a quarter of the sample borrowed money—close to $200,-000—from financial institutions, relatives, or friends during the survey year. Of course, the ability of individuals to adjust to unemployment through borrowing is an indirect reflection of the importance of liquid assets. The ability of family and friends to lend to unemployed persons is obviously a function of their own liquid-asset holdings, and loans from financial institutions are more readily obtainable if the borrower has some liquid assets. Thus these two major adjustive techniques ultimately reinforce one another.

Measured in terms of dollar volume and frequency, reduction in food expenditures was the most important measurable expenditure adjustment. The dollar estimate of the gross reduction in food expenditures is almost 80 per cent of the total expenditure adjustments shown. For the 476 households that utilized this technique, the average weekly reduction in food expenditure was over $7. Forgone durable goods expenditures, either in anticipation or as a result of unemployment, may have been large, but their importance could not be ascertained. The reduced expenditures included in Table 7 account for less than 10 per cent of what the reduction in total expenditures must have been, and it is obvious that respondents were completely unable to account for the actual reductions that must have taken place. Table 7 indicates that the sum of all expenditure adjustments that could be measured came to less than $80,000, and Table 1 suggests that the total expenditure adjustment must have been more than $900,000. Unemployment-induced changes in expenditures for major durable goods, vacations, recreation, house furnishings, clothing, medical expenses—in short, for any class of items where expenditures are not continuous—could not be inferred from the basic data because there would not necessarily be any marked decline during the survey year that could be attributed to the onset of unemployment. On the other hand, many respondents indicated that they were spending less for food at the end of the survey year (when one of the family was receiving unemployment compensation) than at the beginning, and the difference could be attributed to the onset of unemployment.

Though net worth adjustments dominate the adjustment pattern, the three most important techniques, both by dollar volume and by relative frequency, include a debt adjustment, a liquid-asset adjustment, and an expenditure adjustment. Among the less important adjustive techniques, liquidation of life insurance, though used relatively rarely, could constitute a substantial offset to lost income. To many who are concerned with future security this may constitute an undesirable method of adjustment, especially when a less drastic adjustment is available. Rather than cash in or cancel their life insurance, individuals can usually borrow on its cash surrender value, thus keeping the policy intact. The borrower has the usual obligation of repaying the loan (or having the loan plus interest charged against the future cash surrender value). To the extent that the unemployed utilized life insurance in this way, they have been included in the "borrow money (all sources)" category.

It is perhaps a measure of the growing importance of the automobile to the American family that delinquencies on rent were more important than on automobiles. It may also be an indication, however, of consumers' knowledge that delinquency on automobile payments will lead to repossession more rapidly than rent delinquency will lead to eviction.

There is evidence that many American consumers view tobacco or alcohol as necessities. Reductions in these items were small in the over-all adjustment, and indeed some of the sample increased their expenditures during the period of unemployment.

Finally, the pervasiveness of the pattern of relative importance, when the sample is diaggregated by a variety of demographic and related variables, is clearly evidenced by the rank correlation analysis in Table A-8.

Effect of Duration of Unemployment on the Specific Pattern of Financial Adjustment

It has been demonstrated that the longer the period of unemployment, the smaller the relative importance of debt and liquid assets as offsets to income reduction. And by inference, the relative importance of expenditure reductions must have been larger.

Ideally, one would like to know how many weeks after unemployment each individual resorted to the various possible adjustments, since thereby one could measure the priority accorded to them. This adjustment pattern cannot be measured precisely because it is not known how many weeks after unemployment each technique was used initially by each case. However, the sample can be classified by the length of the unemployment period, and the change in the percentage who utilized each technique as the period of unemployment lengthened can be calculated. Evidence of this sort gives some insight into the priority given by the unemployed to each of the techniques under consideration.[5]

The change in the percentage of possible users who utilized selected techniques of adjustment as unemployment lengthens is shown in Table 8. Several difficulties are immediately apparent. The percentages should always increase; no one can be unemployed ten to fourteen weeks without first being unemployed one to nine weeks, and thus the proportion using any given technique should grow unless adjustments are "reversed," which is unlikely. Table 8 indicates that some adjustments are used with reduced frequency as unemployment lengthens. There are two possible explanations: first, the results may be caused by sampling errors, since the number of cases in each cell is small; second, memory error, previously considered, may be responsible.

We have noted that, to the extent a given adjustment affects individual net worth, it is likely to be less destabilizing in the short run than if it leaves net worth intact and changes the stream of expenditures. Probably, therefore, personal loans and life insurance

5 The evidence is summarized in Table A-9.

TABLE 8

CHANGE IN PERCENTAGE OF UNEMPLOYED PERSONS USING SELECTED TECHNIQUES OF ADJUSTMENT, BY DURATION OF UNEMPLOYMENT

Method of Adjustment	Percentage Using Technique During Initial Period of Unemployment, 1-9 Weeks	Change in Percentage Using Technique When Duration of Unemployment Increases to:			Percentage of Total Cases[a]
		10-14 Weeks	15-19 Weeks	20-24 Weeks	
Delinquency					
Rent	10.3	+3.1	+3.9	-2.0	13.9
Mortgage	18.8	+.1	-6.0	+18.6	19.2
Major house improvements	3.9	-2.8	+2.4	-.4	2.9
Appliances					
Purchased during survey year	15.9	+7.3	+8.4	-8.6	24.4
Purchased before survey year	13.6	+16.8	+9.9	-8.0	30.4
Total	16.7	+10.9	+6.3	-9.1	26.8
Hospital payment	3.9	+3.0	+.6	-1.7	5.9
Auto payment	12.6	-6.0	-.3	+7.1	6.9
Repossession					
On auto	4.2	+1.7	-.3	+8.7	6.7
On appliances	0	+2.6	+.2	+.8	3.1
Acquisition of Funds					
Decreasing savings and checking accounts	73.3	-1.4	+2.0	+5.2	73.8
Life insurance loan	1.3	-.3	+.9	+1.4	1.9
Personal loan	23.6	+1.1	-1.4	+1.6	24.6
Sale of auto	4.5	-.2	+5.4	-1.0	7.2

(continued)

Method of Adjustment	Percentage Using Technique During Initial Period of Unemployment, 1-9 Weeks	Change in Percentage Using Technique When Duration of Unemployment Increases to:			Percentage of Total Cases[a]
		10-14 Weeks	15-19 Weeks	20-24 Weeks	
Expenditures					
Food					
Increase	12.7	+.9	-.4	-3.5	13.1
Decrease	28.1	-2.7	+1.5	+.2	25.9
No change	59.2	+1.8	-1.1	+3.3	61.0
Tobacco					
Increase	2.1	-.8	+.4	-.1	1.6
Decrease	5.0	-1.4	+.2	+1.1	3.7
No change	92.9	+2.1	-.5	-1.1	95.0
Liquor					
Increase	8.5	-6.6	+6.6	-5.5	4.8
Decrease	9.8	+1.2	+2.1	-3.6	10.8
No change	81.7	+5.4	-8.7	+9.2	84.4
Movies and recreation					
Decrease	3.8	-1.8	+1.1	+.9	3.1
Newspapers, etc.					
Decrease	2.1	-.6	+.1	+.3	1.6
Auto operations					
Increase	8.6	+4.0	-1.3	-1.3	10.7
Decrease	12.2	-1.0	+4.8	-.5	12.8
No change	79.2	-3.0	-1.0	+1.9	76.6

SOURCE: Derived from Table A-9.

NOTE: Figures are changes in percentage of possible users, not total sample.

[a] Data include those unemployed for more than twenty-six weeks. Since these cases must have experienced more than one period of unemployment during the survey year, they are not analyzed in the table.

loans would interfere less with both effective demand and investment plans than other adjustments. One might argue that delinquency on instalment obligations might adversely affect lender
confidence, though when and to what extent is not known.

The clues to the priority pattern in Table 8 involve consideration
of those techniques that show an increase in frequency as unemployment continues, i.e., those techniques which show plus signs
in the middle three columns. On the basis of the available evidence, it appears that two of the three most important techniques
(decreasing food expenditures and obtaining personal loans) are
both resorted to promptly—indeed, most individuals who use them
at all use them in the first weeks of unemployment. Beyond this,
it seems that adjustments used with increasing frequency up to a
period of twenty weeks of unemployment include delinquencies
and repossessions on appliances, delinquencies on hospital payments, and decreases in automobile expenditures. Techniques which
show an increase only after unemployment has continued for twenty
weeks or more include permitting delinquent mortgage payments
and repossession of automobiles. Selling automobiles rises somewhat earlier, in the fifteen- to nineteen-week interval. Other possible offsets to reduced income show no tendency to be used more
frequently as the period of unemployment lengthens. It is noteworthy that of the three techniques which have previously been
shown to be most important quantitatively, only one—reducing
savings and checking accounts—shows a modest tendency to be used
with increased frequency as the period of unemployment lengthens.
This may be because of the predisposition of a few individuals
to maintain their net worth position as long as possible.

While the dollar volume represented by each adjustment is not
indicated, it is clear from the frequency distribution that household adjustments are a combination of necessity and choice, with
the latter being gradually diminished in importance as unemployment duration lengthens. Under these circumstances, the unemployed have increasingly less flexibility and adjustments become less
and less matters of choice. Mortgage delinquencies are a case in
point. After twenty weeks many can no longer avoid this method
of limiting the drain on reduced resources, and the risk of fore-

closure becomes unavoidable.[6] The rise in automobile repossessions among those unemployed for a long time reflects an earlier rise in the delinquency rate.

Interestingly, the general pattern of relative importance pervades all duration classes. That is to say, if one asks which techniques unemployed individuals favor, the answer does not change materially with the length of their unemployment—only with the degree to which alternative adjustments are utilized. A rank correlation analysis for the eighteen adjustments previously considered showed that the ordering within each unemployment duration class is remarkably similar.[7] If the relative importance is measured as the dollar volume represented by each adjustment, the conclusion is unchanged.[8]

[6] Mortgage delinquencies, as has been noted, may be a calculated risk. Lenders may be willing to permit such delinquencies for short periods of unemployment, knowing that payments are likely to be resumed shortly, and borrowers may anticipate that lenders are reluctant to resort to foreclosure.

[7] The rank correlation coefficients relating to duration of unemployment in Table A-8 are all well over .90 except the 30-weeks-and-over group, which, as previously explained, is largely made up of individuals unemployed more than once during the survey year.

[8] See Table A-8 for the rank correlation coefficients relating frequency of use and dollar volume to duration of unemployment.

IV

FACTORS
AFFECTING THE ADJUSTMENTS
TO UNEMPLOYMENT

Presence or Absence of Liquid Assets
at Beginning of Survey Year

MANY INDIVIDUALS in the sample, it has been remarked, relied heavily upon liquid assets to cushion the impact of unemployment upon their expenditures. It will be of value to break the total sample down into those with and those without liquid assets at the beginning of the survey year. The results (Table 9) show clearly the influence of liquid-asset holdings on the character of the adjustments made by households coping with unemployment.

Average expenditure reductions are markedly larger for those without liquid assets at the start of the survey year, and expenditure reductions for this group invariably are a larger part of income reductions in each unemployment duration class. Indeed, a larger percentage of the income change reflects expenditure reduction by those who have been unemployed less than nine weeks and have no liquid assets than by those unemployed more than twenty-four weeks who possess liquid assets on which to fall back.

The pattern of change in the marginal propensity to consume is as it was in Table 2, except that the MPC is invariably greater in comparable duration classes with no liquid assets. It is worth noting that there is some relation between the presence or absence of liquid assets and the size of the income reduction. Apparently,

AMONG UNEMPLOYED PERSONS, BY DURATION OF UNEMPLOYMENT

Duration of Unemployment (Weeks)	Number in Sample (1)	Average Dollar Change		Average Dollar Offset to Income Reduction		Estimated Marginal Propensity to Consume (6)	Estimated Marginal Propensity to Dissave (7)
		Household Take-Home Pay [a] (2)	Consumption Expenditures [b] (3)	Debt Increase [c] (4)	Liquid-Asset Decrease [d] (5)		
NO BEGINNING-YEAR ASSETS							
0–9	124	−296	−235	66	−6	.79	.21
10–14	178	−442	−350	96	−4	.79	.21
15–19	177	−609	−548	61	0	.90	.10
20–24	146	−819	−734	114	−29	.90	.10
Over 24	214	−1,184	−1,126	70	−13	.95	.05
Total	839	−711	−640	81	−10	.90	.10
SOME BEGINNING-YEAR ASSETS [f]							
0–9	168	−345	−10	85	250	.03	.97
10–14	219	−511	−186	106	218	.36	.64
15–19	210	−772	−276	91	404	.36	.64
20–24	175	−945	−576	88	281	.61	.39
Over 24	225	−1,404	−1,031	76	297	.73	.27
Total	997	−816	−435	90	291	.53	.47
TOTAL SAMPLE							
0–9	292	−324	−106	77	142	.33	.67
10–14	397	−480	−260	102	118	.54	.46
15–19	387	−697	−401	78	219	.57	.43
20–24	321	−888	−648	100	140	.73	.27
Over 24	439	−1,297	−1,077	73	146	.83	.17
Total	1,836	−768	−528	86	154	.69	.31

NOTE: Details may not add to totals owing to rounding.

[a] Inclusive of unemployment compensation payments received during unemployment.

[b] Estimated as a residual (column 2 minus column 4 minus column 5). See discussion in text.

[c] Net increase during the survey year in money borrowed and in unpaid bills, plus nonpayment of instalment obligations because of delinquency or repossession. See discussion in text.

[d] A decrease in liquid assets is positive offset; an increase is a negative offset.

[f] Information on liquid-asset holdings of most households was not obtained, only the change in such assets. For these households, it is assumed that a report of no change means the absence of asset holdings at the beginning of the survey year. For about one-fifth of the sample, liquid-asset holdings were obtained at both the beginning and the end of the survey year. (This was in Pittsburgh and will be analyzed below.) The small increases (negative signs) in liquid-asset adjustments shown in column 5 result from the fact that a few of the Pittsburgh households reporting no assets at the beginning of the survey year held some at the end of the year.

those without liquid assets have smaller income reductions, which no doubt reflects smaller income when employed.[1] There is also some suggestion that households with assets utilize debt to a greater extent than those without during the earlier part of unemployment. After fourteen weeks of unemployment the average debt increase declines, though this may in part be the result of diminished accessibility to further credit along with the necessity of repaying credit obtained during the early period of unemployment.

SIZE OF ASSETS

While there is no information that indicates the levels of beginning-year assets for the entire sample, there are data on these levels for the cases in the Pittsburgh survey.[2]

Table 10 shows these cases classified by beginning-year assets and, within asset groups, by duration-of-unemployment class. It is interesting to note that not only is the average income loss greater as unemployment lengthens, but the previous view that asset holdings are positively correlated with income is corroborated—the higher the asset level, the greater the average income loss within duration classes. Furthermore, the higher the asset level at the beginning of the year, the smaller the average change in consumption expenditure within duration classes. (Indeed, for short periods of unemployment and large assets, there is even a small average in-

---

[1] It is possible that households in the no-liquid-asset category are typically a group with a history of recurrent unemployment. A BLS survey of workers unemployed five weeks or more in 1961 revealed that 22 per cent of those surveyed had been unemployed during each of the previous four years. See Department of Labor, *Monthly Report on the Labor Force*, March 1963, Table 7.

[2] That the Pittsburgh sample does not diverge unduly from the rest of the sample can be seen by these comparisons:

	Pittsburgh	All Cases
Average decrease in income during survey year	$804	$768
Average increase in debt	52	86
Average decrease in liquid assets	131	154
Average decrease in consumption (residual)	621	528
Estimated marginal propensity to consume	.77	.69

TABLE 10
UNEMPLOYMENT-INDUCED CHANGES IN INCOME, EXPENDITURES, DEBT, AND LIQUID ASSETS AMONG 319 UNEMPLOYED PERSONS, BY DURATION OF UNEMPLOYMENT

Duration of Unemployment (weeks)	Number in Sample	Average Dollar Change		Average Dollar Offset[a] to Income Reduction		Estimated Marginal Propensity to Consume	Components of Estimated Marginal Propensity to Dissave	
		Household Take-Home Pay	Consumption Expenditures	Debt Increase	Liquid-Asset Decrease		Debt Change	Asset Change
NO BEGINNING-YEAR ASSETS								
Under 19	98	-468	-421	49	-2	.90	.10	-.00
20 and over	76	-1,030	-1,047	71	-88	1.02	.07	-.08
Total	174	-713	-694	59	-40	.97	.08	.56
BETWEEN $1 AND $500 BEGINNING-YEAR ASSETS								
Under 19	43	-503	-344	24	135	.68	.05	.27
20 and over	34	-1,117	-943	62	113	.84	.06	.10
Total	77	-774	-608	41	125	.79	.05	.16
OVER $500 BEGINNING-YEAR ASSETS								
Under	34	-607	+54	42	619	-.08	.07	1.02
20 and over	34	-1,534	-952	52	530	.62	.03	.35
Total	68	-1,071	-749	47	574	.42	.04	.54

NOTE: Details may not add to totals owing to rounding.

[a] Since debt increases or asset reductions constitute "offsets" to reduced incomes, they are designated by plus signs. Minus signs indicate debt reductions or asset increases.

crease in expenditures, perhaps partly the result of increased leisure time.) Debt adjustment seems to be independent of beginning-year liquid-asset holdings, although the magnitude of the adjustment is positively correlated with duration of unemployment. The result of the combined asset and debt adjustments on the residual expenditures shows up in striking fashion in the estimated marginal propensities to consume. Without exception the MPC's are lower the larger are beginning-year assets for all duration groups, and within asset groups the MPC's rise as unemployment lengthens just as was the case for the entire sample.

Influence of Prior Debt and Duration of Unemployment on the Role of Liquid Assets

Liquid assets can be related to the level not only of beginning-year assets (as in Table 10) but also beginning-year debt. Table 11 considers both of these factors in conjunction with duration of unemployment. Those who have debt outstanding at the beginning of the survey year use up a larger percentage of their assets (of whatever size) than those without debt during comparable periods. By the time unemployment had gone on for as long as twenty-five weeks, households with debt had virtually exhausted their asset holdings, and those in the same duration category who had no debt had consumed only about 40 per cent of their assets. Similar differences appear in other duration-of-employment classes.

This finding is not easy to interpret. It could be a reflection of the financial drain presented by outstanding obligations, thus suggesting that when unemployed individuals can no longer meet debt repayments through income, they are forced to decrease liquid assets. On the other hand, the pattern could simply reflect differences in family preferences for maintaining current consumption at the expense of net worth. Those with prior debt may have a stronger preference for consumption, hence be more willing to use liquid assets in order to maintain consumption during periods of unemployment.[3]

[3] As will be clear from the discussion of Table 12, both those with and without prior debt incurred or increased debt during the survey year, so that changes in debt do not affect the explanations considered here.

TABLE 11

RATIO OF LIQUID-ASSET CHANGE TO BEGINNING-YEAR ASSET LEVEL

Duration of Unemployment (weeks)	Number in Sample (1)	Liquid Assets at Beginning of Survey Year (dollars) (2)	Change in Liquid Assets During Survey Year (dollars) (3)	Reduction in Liquid Assets[a] (per cent) (4)
		SOME ASSETS, SOME DEBT		
0–14	22	13,020	−5,874	45.1
15–24	24	15,250	−13,023	85.4
25 and over	11	4,801	−4,719	98.3
Total	57	33,071	−23,616	71.4
		SOME ASSETS, NO DEBT		
0–14	31	20,050	−6,176	30.8
15–24	31	14,215	−4,130	29.0
25 and over	26	16,639	−6,576	39.5
Total	88	50,904	−16,882	33.2
		TOTAL SAMPLE		
0–14	53	33,070	−12,050	36.4
15–24	55	29,465	−17,153	58.2
25 and over	37	21,440	−11,295	52.7
Total	145	83,975	−40,498	48.2

NOTE: Included in the sample are the 145 individuals in the Pittsburgh sample who had some liquid assets at the beginning of the survey year.

[a] Column 4 is column 3 divided by column 2.

The relations found between asset, debt, and expenditure change as unemployment continues seem strongly pervasive. The effect of both assets and duration of unemployment in combination is impressive—in Table 10 the marginal propensity to consume for those unemployed a short period but having liquid assets over $500 at the beginning of the survey year is actually negative, indicating an increase in consumption. At the other extreme is the MPC of over 100 per cent for those with no assets at the beginning of the year who were unemployed for a long period, implying that expenditures decreased more than income. In between, the combined effects of these two important conditions of adjustment to unemployment produce predictable results, given the variables analyzed.[4]

[4] The multiple correlation analysis for the Pittsburgh data, which is statistically more rigorous, shows precisely this result. See below.

Presence or Absence of Debt at Beginning
of Survey Year

To what extent does beginning-year outstanding debt constitute a source of flexibility in adjusting family spending to lower income brought on by unemployment? Table 12 is comparable to Table 9, except that the sample is divided into those with and those without beginning-year debt. A priori, one might argue that the household already in debt has somewhat less flexibility in coping with unemployment because it is already committed to a schedule of debt repayment. (That this has an effect on the use of liquid assets has already been noted in Table 11.) However, preunemployment expenditures are already compressed below income in that case, and the household has additional options—allowing instalment debt to become delinquent and durable goods to be repossessed. Further, a typical household with debt may well be considered a better credit risk than one without, and some debt-free households may have a distinct aversion to the use of debt as a means of coping with unemployment.

It is clear from Table 12 that, while offsetting factors may be at work, households without debt at the beginning of the year rely less heavily upon debt increases as a way of adjusting to unemployment. Asset changes are about the same for the two groups. In the group with some beginning-year debt, there is an indication that heavy reliance on debt adjustments is associated with less reliance on asset adjustments, although the evidence is not clear-cut. The marginal propensity to consume rises with the duration of unemployment for both the some- and no-debt groups, and the differences appear to be random rather than systematic. Thus, no easy generalization can be made about the effect of debt on expenditure adjustments; in some duration classes the MPC is higher for the group without prior debt and in others it is lower.

SIZE OF PRIOR DEBT

Classification according to size of beginning-year debt (Table 13, Pittsburgh sample only), however, suggests that expenditure

Table 12

Unemployment-Induced Changes in Income, Expenditures, Debt, and Liquid Assets, Unemployed Persons With and Without Debt, by Duration of Unemployment

Duration of Unemployment (weeks)	Number in Sample	Average Dollar Change		Average Dollar Offset to Income Reduction		Estimated Marginal Propensity to Consume	Components of Estimated Marginal Propensity to Dissave	
		Household Take-Home Pay	Consumption Expenditures	Debt Increase	Liquid-Asset Decrease		Debt Change	Asset Change
NO BEGINNING-YEAR DEBT								
0–9	158	−304	−86	56	161	.28	.18	.53
10–14	218	−451	−266	64	122	.59	.14	.27
15–19	219	−662	−377	70	215	.57	.11	.32
20–24	179	−836	−681	66	90	.82	.08	.11
Over 24	257	−1,225	−1,004	69	152	.82	.06	.12
Total	1,031	−733	−518	66	150	.71	.09	.20
BEGINNING-YEAR DEBT								
0–9	134	−349	−129	101	119	.37	.29	.34
10–14	179	−515	−252	149	114	.49	.29	.22
15–19	168	−743	−431	87	225	.58	.12	.30
20–24	142	−953	−607	143	203	.64	.15	.21
Over 24	182	−1,398	−1,182	80	137	.85	.06	.10
Total	805	−812	−542	111	159	.67	.14	.20

NOTE: Details may not add to totals owing to rounding.

TABLE 13

UNEMPLOYMENT-INDUCED CHANGES IN INCOME, EXPENDITURE, DEBT, AND LIQUID ASSETS, BY LEVEL OF BEGINNING-YEAR DEBT AND DURATION OF UNEMPLOYMENT, PITTSBURGH SAMPLE OF UNEMPLOYED PERSONS

Duration of Unemployment (weeks)	Number in Sample	Average Dollar Change		Average Dollar Offset to Income Reduction		Estimated Marginal Propensity to Consume	Components of Estimated Marginal Propensity to Dissave	
		Household Take-Home Pay	Consumption Expenditures	Debt Increase	Liquid-Asset Decrease		Debt Change	Asset Change
NO BEGINNING-YEAR DEBT								
Under 19	104	-467	-316	53	98	.68	.11	.21
20 and over	87	-1,162	-1,069	46	47	.92	.04	.04
Total	191	-784	-659	50	75	.84	.06	.10
BETWEEN $1 AND $500 BEGINNING-YEAR DEBT								
Under 19	42	-490	-333	21	137	.68	.04	.28
20 and over	33	-1,103	-838	47	217	.76	.04	.20
Total	75	-760	-555	32	172	.73	.04	.23
OVER $500 BEGINNING-YEAR DEBT								
Under 19	29	-653	-254	31	369	.39	.05	.56
20 and over	24	-1,290	-971	155	163	.75	.12	.13
Total	53	-941	-579	87	276	.62	.09	.29
Total	319	-804	-621	52	131	.77	.06	.16

NOTE: Details may not add to totals owing to rounding.

adjustments (as measured by the marginal propensity to consume) are related to beginning-year debt level, although the relation is somewhat less strong than that between expenditure adjustment and beginning-year assets. Interestingly enough, the main reason why this type of debt is related to MPC is that debt level and liquid-asset adjustments are strongly correlated—the higher is debt, the larger is the liquid-asset adjustment.

Classification of the sample by unemployment duration and level of beginning-year debt reveals contrasting behavior in the liquid-asset and debt components of the marginal propensity to dissave. The liquid-asset component is always smaller in the longer-duration category irrespective of the level of beginning-year debt. The debt component is smaller in that class in the no-beginning-year-debt category and larger in the $500-and-over category.

Most of these differences reflect the fact that among duration categories income changes tend to be proportionally larger than changes in either debt or asset adjustments; the pattern of the MPC's is thus dominated by the income changes. The only clear-cut relations involving the size of asset and debt adjustments within beginning-year debt and unemployment duration categories are that (1) asset adjustments tend to be larger as the level of beginning-year debt increases (presumably because the levels of beginning-year asset and debt holdings are positively correlated), and (2) the combination of long unemployment duration and large amounts of beginning-year debt is associated with a large debt adjustment. (This is presumably because the frequency of delinquency and repossession increases sharply with both duration and amount of outstanding debt. Alternatively, one might argue that individuals with large beginning-year debt are more prone to utilize debt even in the absence of unemployment, and so to rely on it heavily as unemployment pressures on the household budget increase.)

In the last-mentioned category, the large debt adjustment is associated with a relatively small asset adjustment. This association does not appear to represent voluntary offsetting, i.e., a deliberate decision to limit asset adjustments in favor of debt adjustment. From Table 11, it is clear that households with large amounts of debt, unemployed for a long period, hold a relatively small amount

TABLE 14

UNEMPLOYMENT-INDUCED CHANGES IN INCOME, EXPENDITURE, DEBT, AND LIQUID ASSETS OF UNEMPLOYED PERSONS, BY PRESENCE OR ABSENCE OF BEGINNING-YEAR DEBT AND ASSETS AND BY DURATION OF UNEMPLOYMENT

Duration of Unemployment (weeks)	Number in Sample	Average Dollar Change		Average Dollar Offset to Income Reduction		Estimated Marginal Propensity to Consume	Components of Estimated Marginal Propensity to Dissave	
		Household Take-Home Pay	Consumption Expenditures	Debt Increase	Liquid-Asset Decrease		Debt Change	Asset Change
SOME ASSETS, SOME DEBT								
0–9	83	−355	−46	117	192	.13	.33	.54
10–14	101	−548	−180	165	204	.33	.30	.37
15–19	91	−826	−308	101	416	.37	.12	.50
20–24	78	−1,024	−522	131	371	.51	.13	.36
Over 24	95	−1,491	−1,127	100	264	.76	.07	.18
Total	448	−852	−442	123	287	.52	.14	.34
SOME ASSETS, NO DEBT								
0–9	85	−336	+24	53	306	.07	.16	.91
10–14	118	−479	−192	56	230	.40	.12	.48
15–19	119	−730	−252	84	395	.34	.12	.54
20–24	97	−882	−619	54	208	.70	.06	.24
Over 24	130	−1,340	−961	59	320	.72	.04	.24
Total	549	−786	−429	+62	295	.54	.08	.38

(continued)

Duration of Unemployment (weeks)	Number in Sample	Average Dollar Change		Average Dollar Offset to Income Reduction		Estimated Marginal Propensity to Consume	Components of Estimated Marginal Propensity to Dissave	
		Household Take-Home Pay	Consumption Expenditures	Debt Increase	Liquid-Asset Decrease[a]		Debt Change	Asset Change
NO ASSETS, SOME DEBT								
0–9	51	-339	-264	75	0.0	.78	.22	.00
10–14	78	-472	-345	128	-1.3	.73	.27	b
15–19	77	-645	-575	70	-.1	.89	.11	b
20–24	64	-867	-710	158	-.9	.81	.18	b
Over 24	87	-1,296	-1,241	57	-2.4	.96	.04	b
Total	357	-762	-667	96	-1.0	.88	.13	b
NO ASSETS, NO DEBT								
0–9	73	-266	-214	60	-8.2	.80	.23	-.03
10–14	100	-419	-354	72	-7.0	.84	.17	-.02
15–19	100	-582	-527	55	0.0	.91	.09	-.00
20–24	82	-782	-753	80	-5.7	.96	.10	-.01
Over 24	127	-1,107	1,048	79	-19.7	.95	.07	-.02
Total	482	-673	619	70	-16.5	.92	.10	-.02

[a] The small negative offsets come exclusively from the Pittsburgh sample, in which liquid assets were reported in a different and more inclusive measure.

[b] Less than .005.

of liquid assets; hence they do not have the option of reducing assets by as much as households unemployed for shorter periods of time.

Interaction of Factors Affecting Adjustment to Unemployment

All these relationships can be seen in Table 14, which classifies the entire sample by the presence or absence of beginning-year liquid assets and debt. The status of beginning-year assets is clearly the most important influence on the size of expenditure adjustments; debt position at that time has a less clear-cut effect on subsequent expenditure reductions. Further, those with both assets and debt tend to acquire more debt than other households, thus maintaining expenditures to a greater degree than any other group in the sample.

Multivariate regression analysis (of the Pittsburgh cases) gives further insight into the relationships just described. The variables follow:

Dependent Variables

ΔD Dollar change in unemployment-induced debt, survey year
ΔA Dollar change in assets, survey year
ΔC Dollar change in consumption expenditures, survey year
$\Delta C/\Delta Y$ Marginal propensity to consume

Independent Variables

Y Annual household income prior to unemployment, dollars
U Duration of unemployment, weeks
P_1 Beginning-year debt-asset position: some assets, some debt $= 1$, all other households $= 0$
P_2 Beginning-year debt-asset position: some assets, no debt $= 1$, all other households $= 0$
P_3 Beginning-year debt-asset position: no assets, some debt $= 1$, all other households $= 0$
P_4 Beginning-year debt-asset position: no assets, no debt $= 1$, all other households $= 0$

D_{t-1} Beginning-year outstanding debt on durable goods, dollars
L_{t-1} Beginning-year money loans outstanding, dollars
A_{t-1} Beginning-year liquid-asset holdings, dollars
E Expectation of unemployment: 1 = expected unemployment, 0 = did not expect unemployment

INTERACTIONS

L^2_{t-1} Beginning-year money loans, squared
UD_{t-1} Duration of unemployment times beginning-year durables debt
UL_{t-1} Duration of unemployment times beginning-year money loans
UA_{t-1} Duration of unemployment times beginning-year liquid assets

Table 15 summarizes the results. Coefficients are indicated for all variables that showed a reasonable degree of statistical significance at any point in the stepwise regression procedure, in which independent variables were introduced one at a time in the order listed. To avoid overdetermining the system, P_4 was omitted from the independent variables; the coefficients of P_1, P_2, P_3, are thus to be read as differences relative to P_4, the omitted classification.

Net of all independent variables included in the regression, equation 1 indicates that unemployment-induced change in debt (ΔD) is likely to be higher the higher the level of beginning-year durables debt (D_{t-1}) and the lower the level of beginning-year money loans (L_{t-1}). Apparently, the larger the amount of durables debt, the more likely are delinquencies and repossessions to take place, both of which serve to eliminate a drain on current resources. But the larger are beginning-year money loans outstanding, the less likely is the respondent to increase debt, presumably because expansion of loans is more difficult and some repayment must be made. Equation 2 indicates that the relation between beginning-year money loans and the increase in unemployment-induced debt is nonlinear. For those with relatively small amounts of debt the net effect is negative; it is positive for those with large amounts or unemployed for long periods of time.

Equation 3 indicates that the reduction in liquid assets (ΔA) is likely to be larger if one has such assets at the beginning of the survey year—hardly an astonishing result. But the data also suggest that the reduction in liquid assets is likely to be greater for asset holders who also have beginning-year debt (P_1) than for those who

TABLE 15

SUMMARY OF REGRESSION DATA, PITTSBURGH SAMPLE OF 319 UNEMPLOYED PERSONS

(regression coefficients for independent variables and standard errors)

Equation Number	Dependent Variables	Y	U	P_1	P_2	D_{t-1}	L_{t-1}	A_{t-1}	L^2_{t-1}	UI_{t-1}	UA_{t-1}	Constant Term	Multiple R^2
1	ΔD					.140 (.039)	-.163 (.074)					66.6	.082
2	ΔD					.079 (.066)	-.633 (.187)		.0032 (.0020)	.0115 (.0065)		93.4	.110
3	ΔA			-297 (87)	-113 (69)	-.157 (.089)		-.286 (.040)				10.4	.300
4	ΔA			-275 (88)	-87 (69)	-.099 (.151)		-.101 (.072)			-.0125 (.0040)	-94.8	.323
5	ΔC	-.133 (.020)	-29.2 (4.9)			.158 (.137)	-.250 (.259)	.285 (.062)				-551.6	.354
6	ΔC	-.134 (.020)	-32.0 (5.7)			-.385 (.232)	-1.33 (.66)	.190 (.110)		.059 (.023)		-636.9	.371
7	$\Delta C/\Delta Y$	.545 (.234)	-24 (6.3)		-21 (5.0)		.018 (.012)	-.012 (.003)				77.8	.249
8	$\Delta C/\Delta Y$	.545 (.273)	-26 (6.4)		-21 (5.0)		.057 (.031)	.015 (.005)	.00048 (.00034)			77.8	.257

NOTE: The dependent variables have different algebraic signs. ΔD, debt adjustment, tends to be generally positive since the unemployed typically increase their indebtedness relative to the scheduled or normal change. ΔA, asset adjustments, and ΔC, consumption adjustments, are typically negative since the unemployed ordinarily reduce both assets and consumption. The marginal propensity to consume, $\Delta C/\Delta Y$, is generally positive because both consumption and income tend to decline during unemployment.

do not (P_2), and that the asset reduction is apt to be larger the larger are both the amounts of beginning-year durables debt (D_{t-1}) and beginning-year assets (A_{t-1}). This again suggests a complementary relation between the use of debt and assets to maintain expenditures: households that increase debt the most are also apt to decrease assets the most, other things being equal. Equation 4 suggests further that the relation between duration of unemployment and asset reduction is nonlinear, being relatively large for combinations of long periods of unemployment and large amounts of beginning-year assets. Net of this interaction effect, duration by itself appears to have no influence on the amount of asset reduction.

Equation 5 indicates that consumption expenditures are likely to show a greater decrease the larger the beginning-year level of family income (Y), the longer the duration of unemployment (U), the larger the level of beginning-year money loans (L_{t-1}), and the smaller the level of beginning-year liquid assets (A_{t-1}). Equation 6 shows much the same results except that the influence of beginning-year money loans on consumption-expenditure change is apparently nonlinear, along the lines described above in Equation 2.

Finally, the marginal propensity to consume $(\Delta C/\Delta Y)$ is greater (and the marginal propensity to dissave is smaller) the longer the duration of unemployment; the MPC is smaller for those who have beginning-year assets (P_2) and somewhat smaller still for those with beginning-year debts as well (P_1), and it is smaller the larger the amount of beginning-year liquid assets. The level of beginning-year money loans also has some influence, again nonlinear along the lines discussed earlier.

Impact of Beginning-Year Assets on the Pattern of Specific Adjustment

We have thus far considered the impact of the presence or absence of liquid assets and debt on the aggregate adjustments to unemployment. In addition, data on specific adjustments can be examined. It turns out that the rank order for the eighteen adjustments summarized in Table 6 is much the same whether or not the unemployed individuals utilized liquid-asset holdings. The rank correlation coefficient, eliminating the major technique used by those with assets (decreasing them), is +0.89. That is to say, the order of use, measured by frequency, differed only slightly between the two groups.[5] No comparable information is available for the sample classified with and without debt; those without debt at the beginning of the year would necessarily have shown marked differences because, for example, they had no debt to become delinquent.

Impact of Recessions on the Pattern of Adjustment to Unemployment

The data utilized in this study do not lend themselves readily to a study of the impact of the business cycle *per se* on the adjustive techniques utilized by the affected households. The Pennsylvania survey was the only one covering a twelve-month period of recession, and that pilot survey is not always comparable to the other five. We have seen, however, that the results of a study of the Pittsburgh data confirm the general pattern of the results achieved for the entire sample. Unemployment will tend to be longer in periods of recession, and by indirection, therefore, our findings concerning the increasingly pervasive character of the adjustments required as unemployment continues suggest something of the impact of recessions on the character of financial adjustment to unemployment.

Had postwar recessions been characterized by price declines, the dollar volume of the adjustment required for given periods of unemployment might have been smaller during recession periods than during expansion periods. This, of course, has not been the case. Recessions may, therefore, affect the magnitude of the adjustments required because the average duration of unemployment may be longer. While it is possible to argue that widespread unemploy-

[5] In the same way, seven adjustments for which both frequency and dollar-volume information are available were analyzed with a view to seeing whether the presence or absence of liquid-asset holdings affected the results materially. The rank correlation coefficient for those seven adjustments, measured in terms of relative frequency of use, was quite low (.39); but the total dollar volume represented by each technique gave a rank correlation of .93, and when the two were combined to yield average dollar adjustments the two groups were quite close in ordering also (.75).

ment may reduce the pressure on a community so affected to maintain current expenditures during unemployment save for the minimal necessary outlays, we have no data with which to test this hypothesis.

While Pennsylvania was the only state survey conducted during twelve months of recession, there were three (Florida, South Carolina, and New York) conducted during a year of expansion. The survey year in Missouri and Oregon contained four months of expansion and eight of recession. Inasmuch as the average length of unemployment in our sample was slightly over eighteen weeks, this means that in the latter two states the majority of the cases were interviewed during recession. In taking account of the pattern of relative importance, it is possible to consider whether the pattern in Pennsylvania, Missouri, and Oregon showed a higher degree of consistency in contrast to the other three states, where the survey periods were periods of expansion. As the rank correlation coefficients of Table A-8 make clear, no such distinction is discernible. This is not surprising in view of the evidence, also visible in that table, that the duration of unemployment had no impact on the pattern of relative importance.

Finally, spending decisions during unemployment might be affected by expectations of early re-employment. The latter might be better when unemployment occurred during expansion than during recession. In each of the six areas surveyed by the Bureau of Employment Security, the unemployed were questioned about whether or not they thought their chance of re-employment within the next two weeks were "good." The percentage in each area who thought they had good chances of re-employment within the next two weeks was as follows: Pennsylvania, 47.3 per cent; Florida, 19.1 per cent; South Carolina, 30.0 per cent; New York, 20.1 per cent; Missouri, 18.1 per cent; Oregon, 23.4 per cent. From this evidence, it cannot be concluded that the unemployed persons in the areas surveyed during recession saw their possibilities for early re-employment in any less favorable light than did those unemployed during periods of expansion. However, the evidence is too fragmentary to be considered as more than suggestive. In general this study has attempted to analyze the financial adjustments by abstracting from the business cycle. For this purpose, the inclusion of subsamples collected during periods of both expansion and recession was considered to be advantageous.

Conclusions

On the whole, the results suggest that adjustments to unemployment become increasingly destabilizing both to the households and to the economy as the period of unemployment lengthens. The destabilizing effects are least severe to the economy in the short run if the individual makes maximum use of liquid assets and debt —in effect, if he permits his net worth position to deteriorate rather than if he cuts expenditures. The long-run situation is different; the unemployed who allow their net worth position to deteriorate pay a price for maintaining expenditure patterns during the period of unemployment: they lose their assets and burden themselves with debt. When re-employed they must pay off debt and attempt to rebuild their assets, both of which presumably slow down the restoration of normal expenditure patterns.

In sum, unemployed individuals may elect to have the full or a large share of the real burden of unemployment—reduced consumption—fall on themselves and their family immediately, or they may elect to stretch the burden out over a longer period. The evidence suggests that the unemployed typically choose the latter course, and that this choice is one of the factors which may have tended to reduce the severity of cyclical fluctuations in the economy during the postwar period. Both of the preferred adjustments—utilizing debt and reducing liquid assets—help to maintain consumption. Hence their immediate consequences are similar to those of the so-called built-in stabilizers, such as unemployment compensation and reductions in personal income tax liability, that offset declines in money income.

Unemployment compensation payments are quantitatively one of the most important of the stabilizing elements,[6] and have the added advantage of permitting a partial maintenance of consump-

---

[6] For recent information on this topic, see the BLS 1961 *Survey of the Work History of the Unemployed*, August 1963.

tion without requiring a concomitant deterioration in net worth position. Furthermore, unemployment compensation tends to reinforce other methods of adjustment. For example, credit is likely to be more readily available if some regular source of income exists. And unemployment compensation, in turn, helps to preserve the household's liquid-asset position for a longer period.

APPENDIX A

LIMITATIONS OF THE DATA

As has been mentioned in the text, the basic data were developed in the original surveys to test the adequacy of unemployment benefits. The aim of this study has been somewhat broader—to examine the entire range of adjustments which unemployed persons make.

Although there is no reason to question the accuracy with which the interviewers recorded the information they received, there is a serious question about the reliability of the replies to a number of questions. For example, the claimants were asked to give their average monthly expenditures on a large number of items, such as food, liquor, tobacco, clothing, and recreation for each month during the survey year. Since it is questionable whether the average person can recall these details with any degree of accuracy, this study assumes that the claimant would remember approximately when major adjustments were made and about how large they were. There is less confidence in the reporting of other expenditures. The timing of expenditure changes appears to be more accurate than quantitative estimates of the details for months before or after unemployment.

Each individual survey differed from all the other surveys in several important respects.[1] They were not all taken at the same time, the interviewers were much more painstaking in some states than in others, and the states themselves differed widely in their economic and demographic structures. It appears that they were

[1] There is some reason to question the comparability of the Florida data with that obtained in the other state surveys. Originally the differences did not appear to be so great as to warrant excluding the Florida material, but as the analysis for this study proceeded there were many occasions when the relationships indicated by the other five surveys were not observable in the Florida survey.

selected by the Bureau of Employment Security precisely because
of this diversity. This is a virtue in that any trends or tendencies
for certain kinds of adjustments to prevail must be sufficiently
clear to emerge from an analysis of claimants with diverse back-
grounds. Occasionally the results of a specific type of analysis have
been indicated separately for the six surveys, but in general the
surveys have been combined so that what emerges is a pattern
of adjustment to unemployment based on various sorts of people
and covering periods of prosperity as well as recession.

A more serious problem concerns the relation between the basic
data and the conceptually relevant data for a study of adjustments
to unemployment. Ideally, one would like to know the adjustment
in the "normal" rate of spending for consumption, the "normal"
rate of change in debt, the "normal" rate of change in liquid assets, and the "normal" rate of default on instalment credit obligations. Information such as this cannot be obtained from the data
at hand because the characteristics of a normal (not influenced by
unemployment) period are not known for this sample of households.
There is considerable information in the surveys concerning magnitudes (e.g., durable goods instalment debt) held at the beginning
of the survey year, and much concerning how magnitudes were altered during the survey year. But there is no information about
how these magnitudes change normally, e.g., during the year *preceding* the survey year (a year presumably, but not necessarily,
marked by unemployment). Thus the change in several debt categories during the survey year can be computed, but it cannot auto-
matically be said that this change was "associated with unemployment" unless it is assumed that debt normally does not change at
all. Similarly, if there was a 10 per cent increase in unpaid food
bills during the survey year, it would in principle be necessary to
know the change in unpaid food bills during previous years. In
effect, one would like to be able to talk about unemployment-asso-
ciated changes in normal rates of change, i.e., about first differences.

This inability to measure first differences makes it extremely
difficult to interpret some of the data. To relate a change (in tobacco
expenditures, for example) during the survey year entirely to the
existence of unemployment is to imply that the rate of change in

the past had been nonexistent or negligible. In this example the assumption that change is equal to first differences might not lead one too far afield. But to attribute a decrease in liquid assets to unemployment might underestimate the effect of unemployment on saving, since liquid assets may well have tended to increase in "normal" periods. Some indirect evidence can be brought to bear on this pattern, and it has been discussed in the text.

TABLE A-1

AGE DISTRIBUTION OF CIVILIAN LABOR FORCE, UNEMPLOYED PERSONS,
BLS SURVEY OF INSURED UNEMPLOYED PERSONS, AND BES SAMPLE
OF INSURED UNEMPLOYED PERSONS

Age Class	Total Civilian Labor Force, 1956[a] (per cent) (1)	Unemployed Persons, 1956[a] (per cent) (2)	BLS Survey of Insured Unemployed Persons, 1956[b] (per cent) (3)	BES Survey of Unemployed Persons, 1954–58 Per Cent (4)	BES Survey of Unemployed Persons, 1954–58 Number (5)
20–24	9.5	17.4	13.8[c]	8.0	147
25–34	24.0	24.3		28.0	514
35–44	25.2 }49.2	20.7 }44.9	47.3	29.9 }57.9	549
45–54	21.5	18.9		17.4	319
55–64	14.2 }35.7	13.9 }32.7	34.6	10.7 }28.1	196
65 and over	5.5	4.9	4.3	4.4	80
Not ascertained				1.7	31
Total	100.0	100.0	100.0	100.0	1,836

NOTE: Details may not add to totals owing to rounding. Chi-square analysis of column 4 vs. column 2 and column 3 shows that the differences are significant at the .01 per cent level, due largely to the underrepresentation of the two younger classes in the BES sample.

[a] Department of Commerce, *Current Population Reports, Annual Report on the Labor Force*, 1956, Series P-50.

[b] Department of Labor, *Monthly Report on the Characteristics of the Insured Unemployed*, December 1956, Table C-3. This survey is based on a 1 per cent sample of insured unemployed.

[c] This class is "under 25" and is not strictly comparable.

MARITAL STATUS OF U.S. ADULT POPULATION, BLS SURVEY OF INSURED UNEMPLOYED PERSONS, AND BES SAMPLE OF INSURED UNEMPLOYED PERSONS

Marital Status	U. S. Adult Population, 1958[a] (per cent)	BLS Sample of Insured Unemployed Persons, 1956[b] (per cent)	BES Sample of Unemployed Persons, 1954–58	
			Per Cent	Number
Single	21.6	18.5	26.2	481
Married	78.4	73.2	73.7	1,353
		81.5		
Widowed		8.3	0.0	0
Divorced			0.1	2
Total	100.0	100.0	100.0	1,836

[a] Department of Commerce, Bureau of the Census, *Current Population Reports,* Series P-20, No. 87. Reproduced in *Statistical Abstract of the United States,* 1959, p. 40.

[b] Department of Labor, *Monthly Report on the Characteristics of the Insured Unemployed,* December 1956, Table A-7.

OCCUPATIONAL DISTRIBUTION OF EXPERIENCED CIVILIAN LABOR FORCE, UNEMPLOYED PERSONS IN EXPERIENCED CIVILIAN LABOR FORCE, BLS SURVEY OF INSURED UNEMPLOYED PERSONS, AND BES SURVEY OF UNEMPLOYED PERSONS

Occupation	Total U.S. Experience Civilian Labor Force, 1954–58[a] Average (per cent)	Unemployed Persons in Experienced Civilian Labor Force, 1956[b] (per cent)	BLS Survey of Insured Unemployed Persons, 1956[c] (per cent)	BES Survey of Unemployed Persons, 1954–58 Per Cent	Number
Professional, semi-professional, and managerial	19.3[d]	5.0[d]	2.9	2.6	47
Clerical and sales	19.8	14.5	11.0	10.8	199
Skilled and semiskilled	33.4	44.7	45.0	36.0	661
Unskilled and service	17.8	30.4	37.8	47.4	871
Agricultural workers	9.5	5.6	—	1.6	29
Not ascertained	—	—	3.2	1.6	29
Total	100.0	100.0	100.0	100.0	1,836

NOTE: Details may not add to totals owing to rounding.

[a] Department of Commerce, *Current Population Reports, Annual Report on the Labor Force,* 1954–58, Series P-50.

[b] Estimated by applying annual average (1956) of unemployment rates (experienced unemployed as percentage of experienced civilian labor force) to the distribution of experienced civilian labor force by occupation (1956). Unemployment rates are taken from Table P, p. 10, *1956 Annual Report on the Labor Force,* Series P-50, *Current Population Reports,* Department of Commerce.

[c] Department of Labor, *Monthly Report on the Characteristics of the Insured Unemployed,* December 1956, Table 4. These estimates are an unweighted average of the percentage distribution for those unemployed for one to four weeks and over fourteen weeks. While this does not include all the insured unemployed, it is a better estimate than that of any single month, which is subject to seasonal factors.

[d] Excluding farm managers, who were included with agricultural workers.

TABLE A-4

DISPOSABLE-INCOME DISTRIBUTION OF U.S. POPULATION AND BES SAMPLE OF INSURED UNEMPLOYED PERSONS

Income Class	Percentage Distribution of Consumer Units, Total U.S., 1955-57[a]				BES Sample of Unemployed Persons, 1954-58[b]	
	1955	1956	1957	3-Year Average	Per Cent	Number
Under $2,000	16.8	15.7	14.9	15.8	8.6	157
2 - 2,999	12.5	11.7	11.0	11.7	15.7	289
3 - 3,999	15.3	14.9	13.9	14.7	18.7	344
4 - 4,999	15.7	15.2	14.8	15.2	17.9	329
5 - 5,999	12.8	12.7	12.6	12.7	16.1	295
6,000 and over	26.9	29.8	32.8	29.8	21.4	392
Not ascertained					1.6	30
Total	100.0	100.0	100.0	100.0	100.0	1,836
Median income	$4,338	$4,506	$4,689	$4,513	$4,346	

NOTE: Details may not add to totals owing to rounding.
[a] Department of Commerce, *Survey of Current Business,* April 1959, Table 12.
[b] Data represent household income prior to unemployment.

TABLE A-5

PERCENTAGE OF SPENDING UNITS WITH NO PERSONAL DEBT

Within Income Groups			Within Age Groups		
Income Class	All Spending Units, 1957[a]	BES Sample of Unemployed Persons, 1954-58	Age Class	All Spending Units, 1957[a]	BES Sample of Unemployed Persons, 1954-58
Under $1,000	60	57	18-24	38	22
1 - 1,999	53				
2 - 2,999	49	48	25-34	23	16
3 - 3,999	42	33	35-44	33	25
4 - 4,999	31	24	45-54	42	34
5 - 5,999	33	17	55-64	55	60
6,000	26	17	65 and over	73	80
7,500 and over	34		Not ascertained	--	48
Total	41	30	Total	41	30

[a] Survey of Consumer Finances, *Federal Reserve Bulletin,* September 1958, Supplementary Table 11. The percentages apply to spending units.

Percentage of Spending Units with No Liquid Assets

Within Income Groups			Within Age Groups		
Income Class	All Spending Units, 1957[a]	BES Sample of Unemployed Persons, 1954–48	Age Class	All Spending Units, 1957[a]	BES Sample of Unemployed Persons, 1954–58
Under $1,000	62		Under 25	37	47
– 1,999	50	56	25 – 34	26	40
– 2,999	37	50	35 – 44	22	41
– 3,999	32	45	45 – 54	21	45
– 4,999	25	44	55 – 64	28	50
– 5,999	16	40	65 and Over	27	39
– 7,499	10	28	Total	26	43
7,500 – 9,999	2				
10,000 and Over	1				
Total	26	43			

[a] Survey of Consumer Finances, *Federal Reserve Bulletin,* September 1958, Supplementary Tables 7 and 9. The percentages apply to spending units.

Table A-7

Percentage Distribution of Household Expenditures Within Income Groups for All Households (1955–56) [a] and for the BES Sample of Insured Unemployed Persons (1954–58)

Expenditure Category	Under $2,000		$2,000–2,999		$3,000–3,999		$4,000–4,999		$5,000–6,999		$7,000–9,999		$10,000 and Over	
	All U.S. Households	BES Sample	U.S.	BES	U.S.	BES	U.S.	BES	U.S.	BES	U.S.	BES	U.S.	BES
Food	36	42	33	41	30	42	29	40	28	37	26	36	24	40
Clothing	11	7	11	7	13	7	12	7	11	8	13	8	14	8
Medical	7	3	5	3	6	2	5	2	5	2	5	2	6	2
Home operation	17	32	20	29	18	26	19	24	19	24	18	25	18	18
Home furnishing	7	7	8	8	8	7	8	8	9	8	9	7	10	9
Recreation	5	2	5	2	5	2	6	1	5	2	5	1	6	2
Automotive	3	7	13	11	15	14	14	17	16	19	15	20	15	20
Other	6	—	5	—	6	—	7	—	7	—	9	—	7	—
Total	100	100	100	100	100	100	100	100	100	100	100	100	100	100

RANK OF EXPENDITURE CATEGORY

Expenditure Category	Under $2,000		$2,000–2,999		$3,000–3,999		$4,000–4,999		$5,000–6,999		$7,000–9,999		$10,000 and Over	
	All U.S. Households	BES Sample	U.S.	BES	U.S.	BES	U.S.	BES	U.S.	BES	U.S.	BES	U.S.	BES
Food	1	1	1	1	1	1	1	1	1	1	1	1	1	1
Clothing	3	4	4	5	4	4.5	4	5	4	4.5	4	4	4	5
Medical	4.5	6	6.5	6	6	6.5	7	6	6.5	6.5	6.5	6	6.5	6.5
Home operation	2	2	2	2	2	2	2	2	2	2	2	2	2	3
Home furnishing	4.5	4	5	4	5	4.5	5	4	5	4.5	5	5	5	4
Recreation	6	7	6.5	7	7	6.5	6	7	6.5	6.5	6.5	7	6.5	6.5
Automotive	7	4	3	3	3	3	3	3	3	3	3	3	3	2
Other														
Rank Correlation Coefficient	.72		.98		.98		.92		.99		.99		.92	

[a] *Life* Magazine *Study of Consumer Expenditure*, Volume 1, 1957. The *Life* survey was taken between October 1955 and December 1956. See Volume 1, p. 5, for details of the survey procedure. The *Life* survey deals with annual household income, otherwise unspecified, and so presumably before taxes. The Unemployment Survey sample is based here on after-tax income.

RANK CORRELATION BETWEEN SAMPLE AS A WHOLE AND INDICATED
SUBGROUPS, NINE PRINCIPAL TECHNIQUES OF ADJUSTMENT
TO UNEMPLOYMENT

Subgroup	Rank Correlation Coefficient for:	
	Frequency of Use	Dollar Amount
Age: under 35 years	.96	.93
35 years and over	.996	1.00
Occupation		
Professions etc.	.91	.92
Clerical and sales	.95	.93
Skilled and semiskilled	.93	.92
Unskilled and service	.73	.98
Agricultural	.80	.81
Earner status		
Single	.90	.95
Primary	.93	.95
Secondary	.98	.88
Change in liquid assets		
Negative		
$1,000 and over	.81	.70
$300 - 999	.94	.97
$100 - 299	.94	.97
Under $100	.96	.95
Positive		
Under $1,000	.74	.90
$1,000 and over	.55	.55
Percentage change in income		
Negative		
20 and over	.98	.97
10 - 19	.96	.98
5 - 9	.98	.92
Under 5	.98	.85
Positive		
Under 10	.95	.83
10 and over	.91	.87
Location		
Pennsylvania	.73	.77
South Carolina	.85	.87
Florida	.88	.88
New York	.93	.87
Missouri	.97	.98
Oregon	.93	.93
Duration of unemployment		
1 - 9 weeks	.95	.95
10 - 14 weeks	.95	.97
15 - 19 weeks	1.00	1.00
20 - 24 weeks	.93	.95
25 - 29 weeks	.93	.94
30 weeks and over	.87	.88

TABLE A-9

FREQUENCY OF USE RELATED TO DURATION OF UNEMPLOYMENT, SELECTED ADJUSTMENTS

Method of Adjustment	1-9 Weeks (292 cases)		10-14 Weeks (397 cases)		15-19 Weeks (387 cases)		20-24 Weeks (321 cases)		Total (1,836 cases)[a]	
	Number of Users	Percentage of Possible Users	Number of Users	Percentage of Possible Users	Number of Users	Percentage of Possible Users	Number of Users	Percentage of Possible Users	Number of Users	Percentage of Possible Users
Delinquencies										
Rent	14	10.3	33	13.4	33	17.3	27	15.3	135	13.9
Mortgage	15	18.8	14	18.9	11	12.9	17	31.5	76	19.2
Major house improvements	4	3.9	1	1.1	4	3.5	3	3.1	16	2.9
Appliances										
Purchased during survey year	14	15.9	30	23.2	37	31.6	20	23.0	132	24.4
Purchased before survey year	9	13.6	28	30.4	29	40.3	20	32.3	116	30.4
Total		16.7		27.6		33.9		24.8		26.8
Hospital payment	9	3.9	21	6.9	20	7.5	13	5.8	79	5.9
Auto payment	15	12.6	10	6.6	9	6.3	15	13.4	47	6.9
Repossession										
On autos	5	4.2	9	5.9	8	5.6	16	14.3	46	6.7
On appliances	—	0	4	2.6	4	2.8	4	3.6	21	3.1
Acquisition of funds										
Decrease savings and checking account	132	73.3	151	71.9	153	73.9	140	79.9	737	73.8
Life insurance loans	3	1.3	3	1.0	5	1.9	7	3.3	24	1.9
Personal loans	69	23.7	98	24.7	90	23.2	80	24.9	452	24.6
Sale of automobile	10	4.5	12	4.3	26	9.7	19	8.7	93	7.2

(continued)

Method of Adjustment	1-9 Weeks (292 cases)		10-14 Weeks (397 cases)		15-19 Weeks (387 cases)		20-24 Weeks (321 cases)		Total (1,836 cases)[a]	
	Number of Users	Percentage of Possible Users	Number of Users	Percentage of Possible Users	Number of Users	Percentage of Possible Users	Number of Users	Percentage of Possible Users	Number of Users	Percentage of Possible Users
Change expenditures on:										
Food										
Increase	37	12.7	54	13.6	51	13.2	31	9.7	240	13.1
Decrease	82	28.1	101	25.4	104	26.9	87	27.1	476	25.9
No change	173	59.2	242	61.0	232	59.9	203	63.2	1,120	61.0
Tobacco										
Increase	5	2.1	4	1.3	5	1.7	4	1.6	22	1.6
Decrease	12	5.0	11	3.6	11	3.8	12	4.9	51	3.7
No change	222	92.9	288	95.0	274	94.5	227	93.4	1,309	95.0
Liquor										
Increase	13	8.5	4	1.9	15	8.5	5	3.0	42	4.8
Decrease	15	9.8	23	11.0	23	13.1	16	9.5	95	10.8
No change	125	81.7	182	87.1	138	78.4	148	87.6	743	84.4
Movies and recreations										
Decrease	11	3.8	8	2.0	12	3.1	13	4.0	56	3.1
Newspapers, etc.										
Decrease	6	2.1	6	1.5	6	1.6	6	11.9	30	1.6
Auto Operations										
Increase	19	8.6	35	12.6	23	8.6	16	7.3	127	10.7
Decrease	27	12.2	31	11.2	43	16.0	34	15.5	164	12.8
No change	176	79.2	212	76.3	203	75.3	169	77.2	983	76.6

[a] The sum of cases will not add to the total because of cases involving more than twenty-six weeks of unemployment; these cases must have been employed more than once during the survey year because none of the states covered here paid benefits for more than twenty-six consecutive weeks.

APPENDIX B

DEPENDENT VARIABLES
(ADJUSTIVE TECHNIQUES)
FOR WHICH DATA
WERE AVAILABLE

1. Delinquent rent
2. Rent due at the end of the survey year
3. Number with room and board delinquent
4. Mortgages renewed or refinanced
5. Delinquency on house taxes or insurance
6. Delinquency still in existence at end of survey year
7. Delinquency on major home improvements
8. Amount owed on these home improvements at end of survey year
9. Delinquency on minor home improvements
10. Amount owed on these at end of survey year
11. Amount owed on utilities at end of survey year
12. Amount owed on laundry and dry cleaning at end of survey year
13. Delinquency on appliances purchased during survey year
14. Amount owed on these at end of survey year
15. Delinquency on appliances purchased before survey year but with payments due during survey year
16. Amount owed on these appliances at end of survey year
17. Repossession on all appliances with payments due during survey year

18. Decline in monthly food expenditures during survey year
19. Percentage decline in food expenditures
20. Amount overdue on food bills at end of survey year
21. Decline in tobacco expenditures
22. Percentage decline during period of unemployment
23. Decline in liquor expenditures
24. Percentage decline in liquor expenditures during period of unemployment
25. Amount owed at end of survey year on clothing expenditures
26. Amount owed on clothing purchased before survey year but paid for during survey year
27. Delinquency on hospitalization insurance
28. Hospital plans dropped during survey year
29. Amount owed on autos purchased during survey year
30. Amount owed on autos purchased before survey year but with payments due during survey year
31. Delinquency on auto purchases during survey year
32. Number of months of delinquency reported during survey year
33. Repossession of automobiles during survey year
34. Decline in amount spent on operation of car
35. Amount owed on automobile operations and repair at end of survey year
36. Life insurance
    a. Canceled
    b. Cashed in
    c. Borrowed on
    d. Any of above (summation of a through c)
37. Money borrowed by the family
38. Amount of money borrowed
39. Amount owed on all loans at end of survey year
40. Absolute amount of change in total indebtedness for consumption expenditures
41. Percentage change in the amount of indebtedness for consumption expenditures
42. For major improvements
43. For minor improvements

44. For appliances
45. For automobile purchase
46. Clothing
47. Change in savings and checking accounts during survey year